FREE THINGS FOR
GARDENERS

FREE THINGS FOR
GARDENERS

Kenneth Druse
Edited by Susan Osborn

A Perigee Book

Perigee Books
are published by
G. P. Putnam's Sons
200 Madison Avenue
New York, New York 10016

Edited by Susan Osborn
Text prepared by Barbara Osborn and Tom Cowan
Design: Nancy Swaybill
Research: Garin Wolf
Special thanks to Janine Frontera, & Sam Mitnick

Library of Congress Cataloging in Publication Data

Druse, Kenneth.
Free things for gardeners.

"A Perigee book."
1. Gardening—Equipment and supplies—
Catalogs.   2. Free material—Catalogs.
3. Gardening—Bibliography—Catalogs.   I. Title.
SB454.8.D78   635'.0216   81-15396
ISBN 0-399-50604-7   AACR2

First Perigee printing, 1982

Printed in the United States of America

CONTENTS

I.
Introduction

I can't resist a bargain! I suppose that I'm the original "something for nothing" guy. I always clip and save coupons and record addresses for horticultural offerings —some of which are invaluable, such as the latest government bulletin on biological pest control, and some of which are just for fun, such as the six-foot string beans that I grew from mail-ordered seeds.

As a garden writer, I see some pretty amazing offerings drifting across my desk, and I'm quick to pounce on a good deal. I now get a free lawn and garden care magazine, and many of the seeds I've received as free samples have led to the discovery of a new vegetable favorite. Every January I receive a load of full-color seed and nursery catalogs. These gardening dreambooks announce the first sign of spring, I love to hang the beautiful photographs in the sun room.

Over the years I've amassed quite a hefty collection of names and addresses of companies eager to spread some goodwill, impart good gardening information, and, in many cases, send free samples. I thought it was about time that I and some other gardening aficionados share some of these freebies with you.

Presented within these pages are over 200 names and addresses of companies who want to give you free or nearly free premiums. All the addresses and offerings have been checked and double-checked to ensure that they are accurate and up to date. So get your pencils, paper, envelopes, and stamps ready, and start to receive your *Free Things for Gardeners.*

II.
Seeds:
Vegetables, Herbs, and Flowers

Chives (Allium schoenoprasum)

Vegetable Seeds

J. A. Demonchaux, the French seed importer, offers many seed packets at inexpensive prices. Fin de Bagnol, a gourmet string bean; Petit Provençal, the most popular of the French "petit pois"; Witloof Improved, a Belgian chicory endive; and Green Cambrai, a type of mache mixed with salad greens—all may be obtained directly through Demonchaux for less than $2.00.

Send: Fin de Bagnol #210 $1.35
      Petit Provençal #250   80¢
      Witloof Improved #50   75¢
      Green Cambrai #62   75¢

Ask for: seed packets

Write to: J. A. Demonchaux Co.
      827 N. Kansas
      Topeka, KS 66608

Growing Herbs

It's fun to cook with herbs grown yourself. Here is a book to instruct you on growing 15 common cooking herbs either outdoors or inside. Everything you need to know, from getting plants started to transplanting them. Special-hints sections tell you how to use aromatic herbs as breath fresheners, bathing water scents, sachets, and pot-pourris, how to make herbal tea, and hints for drying herbs. Also, there are charts listing the herbs with appropriate culinary suggestions, medicinal uses, and gift ideas for each.

Send: $2.00

Ask for: "Grow 15 Herbs for the Kitchen" (Garden Way Bulletin A-61)

Write to: Garden Way Publishing
      Dept. A979
      Charlotte, VT 05445

Popcorn

Popping corn has always been a perfect indoor project for kids. Now you can grow your own popcorn and teach nature's life cycle, too. Learn to plant and harvest the corn you'll later pop. Crockett's popcorn flier offers 10 different types of popping corn, as well as culture instructions and recipes.

Send: a self-addressed, stamped envelope

Ask for: popcorn sheet

Write to: The David Crockett Popcorn Co.
P.O. Box 237
Metamora, OH 43540

Save on Seed

Thomas Butterworth of Butterbrooke Farm offers vegetable and herb seeds at just 50¢ per packet. His listings include asparagus, pole beans, beets, broccoli, brussels sprouts, eggplant, kale, kohlrabi, okra, parsnips, pumpkins, and Swiss chard. Other vegetables are also available upon request of a brochure.

Send: 50¢ per packet

Ask for: specify vegetable and free brochure

Write to: Butterbrooke Farm
78 Barry Rd.
Oxford, CT 06483

Potpourri

This introductory herb sampler contains seeds for basil, caraway, chervil, chives, dill, roquette, savory, and sorrel. Create your own "bouquet garni" for perfect French cooking. Great for both the novice and the gardener who wants to dabble in herbs, the offer includes an illustrated catalog featuring herb seeds and plants, planting instructions, cookbooks, gardening books, and recipes.

Send: $1.00

Ask for: catalog and seed samples

Write to: Le Jardin du Gourmet
West Danville, VT 05873

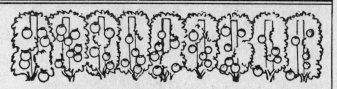

Juicy Tomatoes

Holmes Mexican Tomato Seeds produce unusually large and flat tomatoes. With few seeds and low in acid, this outstanding tomato is Holmes's only product. Simple and thorough organic growing instructions are included, which explain the importance of organic gardening, the different "stem systems" for growing tomatoes, and ideas for companion gardening.

Send: $1.20

Ask for: tomato seeds

Write to: T. Holmes Quisenberry
4626 Glebe Farm Rd.
Sarasota, FL 33580

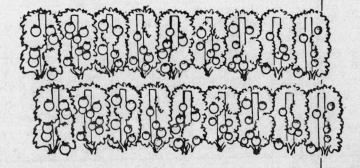

Crockett's Seeds

This 30-page brochure is chock-full of information, charts, and photographs. Crockett offers the traditional vegetables as well as some more unusual items—bean sprouts, Chinese cabbage, and turkey wheat. They also carry herbs and a limited assortment of flowers. All seeds are untreated and guaranteed.

Send: 50¢

Ask for: seed catalog

Write to: Crockett Seed Company
Metamora, OH 43540

Imports

J. A. Demonchaux specializes in French vegetable seeds. Their fascinating catalog includes information on different types of French vegetables (for instance, the difference between "Filets" string beans, and "Mangetout" string beans), and they carry vegetables that are almost unknown in this country—cardoon, French gherkins (cornichons), purslane, and rocket. For the gourmet cook or the adventurous gardener this catalog is a prize.

Send: a postcard

Ask for: vegetable seeds catalog

Write to: J. A. Demonchaux Co.
827 N. Kansas
Topeka, KS 66608

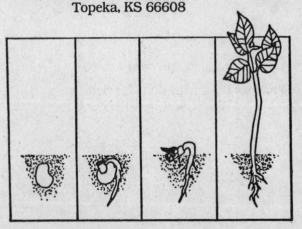

Fresh Vegetables

Only gardeners know what really fresh fruit and vegetables taste like. They know that peak flavor experience and that just-picked freshness. Northrup King's "Basic Vegetable Gardening Guide" tells you how to raise and prepare vegetables with that matchless home-grown taste. The booklet includes chapters on planning, planting and transplanting, organic gardening, and preserving. Also included is a very helpful gardeners' dictionary.

Send: $1.00

Ask for: "Basic Vegetable Gardening Guide"

Write to: Guide
P.O. Box 2966
1 Industrial Dr.
Maple Plain, MN 55359

Seeds for Everyone

This large organization celebrating its 100th birthday leaves nothing to be desired in the way of seeds. Their vegetable offerings are impressive, including common fare as well as collards, cress, peanuts, salsify,

endive, kohlrabi, leeks, and rutabagas. They also have a complete line of flowers handsomely photographed in full color. Another plus for this company is its line of grazing plants: alfalfa, clover, millet, broom corn, and buckwheat.

Send: a postcard

Ask for: catalog

Write to: Wyatt-Quarles Seed Co.
Box 2131
Raleigh, NC 27602

Herb Gardening

This fascinating 40-page booklet was put together by two professors at the New York State College of Agriculture and Life Sciences at Cornell University. It includes general culture information (for indoors or out) and advice on stem-cutting, layering, and division. Other how-to sections discuss drying and storage and herb uses. An excellent key to 50 common herbs is provided, as well as thorough descriptions and photographs of the most popular herbs. Lists of further reading, mail-order seed companies, and a glossary of botanical terms round out the catalog.

Send: $1.25

Ask for: "Gardening with Herbs"

Write to: Distribution Center C
7 Research Park
Cornell University
Ithaca, NY 14850

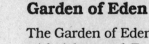

Epicure Seeds

Choice vegetable breeds from Europe are made available to American gardeners through this seed house. The flier offers unusual Belgian and Dutch lettuce, French turnips, German radishes, several breeds of Danish cabbage, as well as certain trial varieties. The catalog also includes planting and serving suggestions.

Send: a postcard

Ask for: 1982 catalog

Write to: Epicure Seeds
Box 69
Avon, NY 14414

Garden of Eden

The Garden of Eden didn't come to an end with Adam and Eve. The Garden of Eden Nursery in Spruce Pine, North Carolina, took inspiration from the original and created a nursery of wonderful plants and flowers. Their catalog features both seeds and plants.

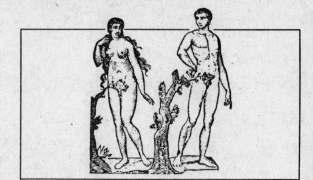

Send: $1.00

Ask for: seed and nursery catalog

Write to: Garden of Eden Nursery
Rt. 2, Box 1086
Spruce Pine, NC 28777

Elephant Garlic

Does elephant garlic sound like an African hybrid? In fact it was developed on a small family farm in northern California. It is a large, mild garlic that the family markets nationwide. Their brochure includes useful recipes for raw, cooked, and pureed elephant garlic, and in addition to their specialty they carry traditional varieties of garlic, onions, comfrey, and shallots.

Send: a large self-addressed, stamped envelope

Ask for: garlic brochure

Write to: S & H Organic Acres
P.O. Box 27F
Fenders Ferry Rd.
Montgomery Creek, CA 96065

Growing Tomatoes

Tomatoes are among the most popular vegetables grown in home gardens. Each plant may be expected to yield eight to 10 pounds of fruit. But you do need to know the proper planting procedures and care for these hardy little plants. This book from the Dept. of Agriculture will give you all the tips and hints to ensure a good crop.

Send: $1.50

Ask for: "Growing Tomatoes in the Home Garden" (Home and Garden Bulletin 187J)

Write to: Consumer Information Center
Dept. Z
Pueblo, CO 81009

Nichols Garden

Gourds come in large and small varieties, the small being the most brilliantly colored. Gourds may be used as ornaments or as rattles, and the unusual luffa gourds may be used for their valuable sponges. Five of Nichols's gourds may be ordered directly.

Luffa Sponge Gourd	85¢ per pack
Dipper Gourd	50¢
Penguin Gourd	50¢
Bird's Nest Gourd	50¢
Dolphin Gourd	50¢

Each order will be accompanied by culture information, with a special fact sheet on the luffa.

Send: price listed

Ask for: specific packet

Write to: Nichols Garden Nursery
1190 N. Pacific Hwy.
Albany, OR 97321

Johnny's Selected Seeds

This Maine-based organization makes its seed selections according to their experience with their trial grounds in one of America's northernmost states. Their catalog is like a grower's handbook, full of information that will prove useful throughout the growing season. Legumes include pinto beans, turtle beans, Maine yellow eye, and soldier beans. The catalog also includes recipes (in the bean section, it's for tofu). A straightforward, no-nonsense catalog for the serious vegetable gardener.

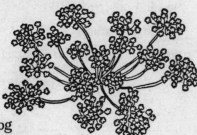

Send: 50¢

Ask for: catalog

Write to: Johnny's Selected Seeds
Organic Seed and Crop Research
Albion, ME 04910

Record Breakers

Grace's Gardens' catalog is a fascinating collection of unique and unusual plants—100-pound pumpkins, yard-long pole beans! Jane Grace works with the *Guiness Book of World Records* searching for the biggest, the longest, the heaviest fruits and flowers in America. Then she includes them all in her "World's Most Unusual Seed Catalog." As a special offer we are listing a few of Grace's enormous products. Many others are available through the catalog.

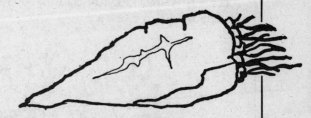

#212 Kyoto Cucumber	$1.00
#214 Armenian Cucumber	$1.20
#162 White Eggplant	$1.20
#144 Jasmine Tobacco	$1.00
#111 Long Radish	$1.00
#120 Ball Carrots	$1.00
# 71 Big Max Pumpkin	$1.00

Send: according to price listed above (free catalog)

Ask for: product or catalog

Write to: Grace's Gardens
10 Bay St.
Westport, CT 06880

Green Thumbers' Paradise

The folks at Lakeland can provide the home gardener with absolutely everything he or she will ever need. It's all here: from shrubs, ground covers, and flowers to fruit trees, edibles, tools, and accessories. Every item backed by a double guarantee of satisfaction. Once you've placed an order, you'll receive this spanking full-color catalog free for the next three years.

Send: $1.00

Ask for: catalog

Write to: Lakeland Nurseries Sales
Hanover, PA 17331

Vegetables and Flowers

Harris's seed catalog includes every common vegetable as well as dozens of different varieties of cabbage, beets, corn (including popcorn and ornamental corn), and yellow and seedless watermelons. They also carry such French favorites as leeks, endive, and the red and white French Horticultural shell beans. They carry an equally large variety of flowers in addition to lawn mixtures and standard gardening tools.

Send: a postcard

Ask for: catalog

Write to: Joseph Harris Co., Inc.
Moreton Farm
Rochester, NY 14624

Seeds

This 75-page seed catalog from Shumway is illustrated with color photographs that will show you what healthy plants should look like and make it easy for you to decide at home what types of flowers and vegetables you should plant this spring. Also included is a comprehensive section on gardening supplies.

Send: a postcard

Ask for: garden catalog

Write to: R. H. Shumway Seedsman
628 Cedar St.
P.O. Box 777
Rockford, IL 61105

More Seeds

The advantage of this 96-page seed catalog is that every so many pages you will discover instructions for planting the more common garden vegetables. There is also a section on growing flowers from seeds.

Send: a postcard

Ask for: "Burrell's Better Seeds"

Write to: D. V. Burrell Seed Growers
P.O. Box 150
Rocky Ford, CO 81067

Nichols Garden

Nichols Garden Nursery offers many vegetable seeds. Their offerings include four kinds of beans, asparagus, dandelion, watercress, Pac-choy, and winter and summer squash. Seed packets come with a helpful planting table, which indicates time to plant, time to harvest, depth to plant, distance between rows, and distance between plants. Also included is a leaflet on insect repellents.

Send: a postcard

Ask for: catalog

Write to: Nichols Garden Nursery
1190 N. Pacific Hwy.
Albany, OR 97321

American Ginseng

When this 1913 Dept. of Agriculture pamphlet on American ginseng first came out, readers were advised that raising this plant for profit depended upon a small Oriental market in the Far East. Today there is greater popular interest in this root, long known for its medicinal properties. In some American circles, using ginseng has become fashionable, particularly among those interested in natural herbs and teas for greater health.

Send: 70¢

Ask for: "The Cultivation of American Ginseng"

Write to: Redwood City Seed Co.
P.O. Box 361
Redwood City, CA 94064

Gardening Is a Family Affair

The Park Seed Co. has a beautiful, full-color catalog—and it's yours for the asking—containing information on the widest selection of flower and vegetable seeds available in the United States. There are tips on how, where, and when to plant, descriptions of tools and accessories that will help your garden grow to its fullest potential, and an order form that makes purchasing seeds, tools, and other materials quick and easy! An index provides information on germination time, best uses, and bloom time for every plant.

Send: a postcard

Ask for: "Park Seed Flowers and
Vegetables"

Write to: Geo. W. Park Seed Co., Inc.
S. C. Hwy. 254 North
Greenwood, SC 29647

Seed Catalog

The Pinetree Seed Co. specializes in small packets of vegetable, flower, and herb seeds at greatly reduced prices. Their philosophy is that many gardeners want smaller seed packets so that they can try many more types of vegetables and flowers in their limited space. Smaller packets often provide as many seeds as most gardeners would want to plant in a given season.

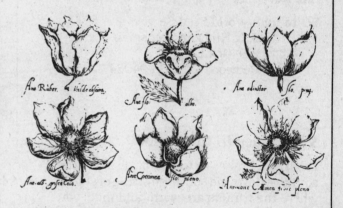

Send: a postcard

Ask for: 1982 seed catalog

Write to: Pinetree Seed Co.
P.O. Box 1399
Portland, ME 04104

An Old-Fashioned Seed Catalog

This old-fashioned seed catalog has just what you would expect: a general seed list, bulk prices, a list of books and societies, vegetable seeds, cactus and succulent seeds, common names index, herb seeds, and germination instructions. You'll like the old look and feel of a traditional almanac with the latest in modern seed ordering.

Send: $1.00

Ask for: "The Complete Catalog of Seeds"

Write to: A World Seed Service
J. L. Hudson, Seedsman
P.O. Box 1058
Redwood City, CA 94064

Digitalis purpurea

Vegetables in the Sunbelt

From San Francisco to Miami, all along the southwestern and southern string of states, where the winters are warm and mild, you can grow vegetables from seeds easily with this handbook arranged by vegetable. Each entry explains how, when, and where to sow and what to expect. Grow your vegetables and save the seeds. Dry them properly to ensure longevity and you'll have even more plants.

Send: $1.25

Ask for: "Vegetable Seed Production in the San Francisco Bay Area of California and Other Warm-Winter Areas of the United States"

Write to: Redwood City Seed Co.
P.O. Box 361
Redwood City, CA 94064

III.
Trees, Shrubs, and Berries

PANICLE

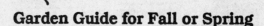

Yarrow

Grafting

Propagating or growing plants by attaching a piece taken from one plant onto another is known as graftage. This differs from making cuttings in that the cut part grows on another plant rather than in the soil where it would produce its own roots. If you have been making cuttings and now would like to do some grafting, learn the difference with this pamphlet that clearly demonstrates bark graft, side graft, cleft graft, and budding.

Send: a self-addressed, stamped envelope

Ask for: "Grafting—An Introduction to the Art"

Write to: Information Officer
West Virginia Dept. of Agriculture
Capitol Building
Charleston, WV 25305

Garden Guide for Fall or Spring

This fall garden guide from Kelly Brothers will colorfully show you the trees, hedges, flowers, and berries that you can order. Free gifts can be had for early orders.

Send: a postcard

Ask for: spring or fall garden guide

Write to: Kelly Brothers
Dansville, NY 14437

shrubs and hedge plants in your overall landscape design.

Send: a self-addressed, stamped envelope

Ask for: "Beginning a Backyard Orchard"

Write to: Information Officer
West Virginia Dept. of Agriculture
Capitol Building
Charleston, WV 25305

Avocado Care

This question-and-answer leaflet will give you lots of information about growing avocados in your own orchard: when to irrigate, how to fertilize, whether to prune and thin the trees, and crucial information about the harvest.

Send: 40¢

Ask for: "Avocado Care in the Home Orchard"

Write to: Redwood City Seed Co.
P.O. Box 361
Redwood City, CA 94064

Backyard Orchards

Yes, even if your backyard is rather small, you can plant an orchard. The development of dwarf and semi-dwarf trees now makes it possible to have an orchard on a plot of land that would have been considered too small for a stand of trees. Apples, peaches, pears, plums, and cherries are now all available either as dwarfs, semi-dwarfs, or both. You can also use these miniature trees to replace

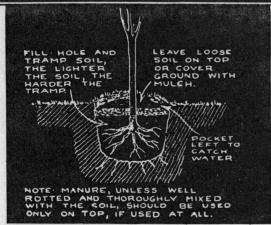

FILL HOLE AND
TRAMP SOIL,
THE LIGHTER
THE SOIL, THE
HARDER THE
TRAMP.

LEAVE LOOSE
SOIL ON TOP
OR COVER
GROUND WITH
MULCH.

POCKET
LEFT TO
CATCH
WATER

NOTE MANURE, UNLESS WELL
ROTTED AND THOROUGHLY MIXED
WITH THE SOIL, SHOULD BE USED
ONLY ON TOP, IF USED AT ALL.

Growing Trees

Many evergreens and other tree seeds may take from two weeks to two years to germinate. During that time drainage is all important. With proper care, trees *will* grow, and Girard Nurseries is happy to explain how. They specialize in growing trees from seed. They carry evergreens, bonsais, yews, Rose of Sharon, and many others. The color catalog includes a description of each tree, and flowering shrubs are often accompanied by a photograph.

Send: a postcard

Ask for: catalog

Write to: Girard Nurseries
P.O. Box 428
Geneva, OH 44041

Just Peaches

Nothing can compare to a peach in sweetness and color. At least peach lovers think so! "Peach Growing" from the New York State College of Agriculture and Life Sciences at Cornell University discusses everything a peach grower needs to know. The discussion includes site and climatic requirements, soil preparation, planting and spacing the trees, and training the young tree. Excellent advice is also provided on the subjects of pruning, thinning and pollination, and picking and packing, as well as a discussion of the different varieties of peaches and their special requirements.

Send: 75¢

Ask for: "Peach Growing"

Write to: Distribution Center C
7 Research Park
Cornell University
Ithaca, NY 14850

Trees, Shrubs, Flowers

Mellinger's of Ohio carries many, many trees and shrubs. They feature dogwood, linden, magnolia, and other seedlings. They also carry native fruit such as buffalo berry, mulberry, choke cherry, and sand cherry. Their unusual fruits and vegetables include kiwis, ginseng, and rice paddies. Mellinger's catalog also contains over 50 pages of tools for every sort of gardener.

Send: a postcard

Ask for: catalog

Write to: Mellinger's, Inc.
2310 W. South Range Rd.
North Lima, OH 44452

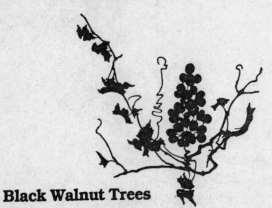

Black Walnut Trees

You can plant black walnut trees for timber with this guidebook from the U.S. Dept. of Agriculture reprint. Much planning and foresight must go into planting these long-term trees. Proper care must extend consistently over the years to ensure you a healthy and profitable stand of trees.

Send: 70¢

Ask for: "Planting Black Walnut for Timber"

Write to: Redwood City Seed Co.
P.O. Box 361
Redwood City, CA 94064

Southern Garden Guide

If you reside south of the Mason-Dixon line, you'll be overjoyed with Hastings's "Southern Garden Guides." Hastings, "Seedsman to the South," offers you this beautiful, illustrated catalog free. It includes varieties of fruits, vegetables, and flowers best suited to the soil and climate of the southern United States, as well as such favorites as pecan, walnut, and almond trees, blueberries, strawberries, raspberries, and blackberries. The catalog also includes instructions for planting each type of plant.

Chestnuts

The chestnut tree was, at one time, an American traditon. Valued for its hard, attractive wood, impervious to decay, and treasured for the delicious flavor of boiled or roasted chestnuts, the chestnut tree was immortalized in Longfellow's poem. Earl Douglas has been in large measure personally responsible for the reemergence of the chestnut tree. He developed a hybrid variety that withstands the fungus that destroyed so many American chestnuts at the turn of the century, and he sells seeds and seedlings of this precious breed.

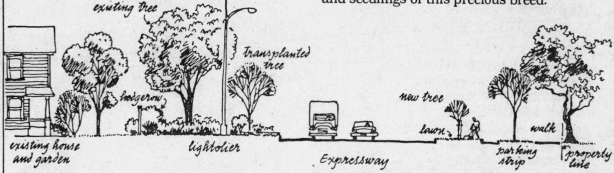

Send: a postcard

Ask for: "Southern Garden Guide"

Write to: H. G. Hastings
Dept. B45
P.O. Box 4274
Atlanta, GA 30302

Send: 25¢

Ask for: chestnut growing brochure

Write to: Earl Douglas
Red Creek, NY 13143

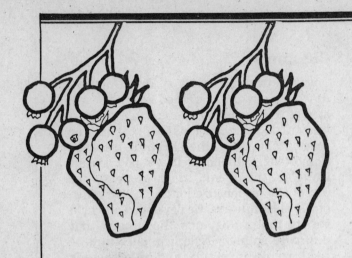

Berries

How many gardeners haven't dreamed of making their own strawberry jam? It's not as difficult as you might think. Although strawberries and raspberries grow best in loamy soil, hardy varieties will thrive in any properly prepared soil. Nourse Farms' catalog offers a description of each of their 24 varieties, a comparative guide to size, resistance, flavor and preservation, soil preparation, planting, and mulching instructions, and crop rotation advice.

Send: a postcard

Ask for: strawberry catalog

Write to: Nourse Farms, Inc.
Box 485, RFD
South Deerfield, MA 01373

Cranberries

This reprint from the Dept. of Agriculture, published in 1903, is a classic on the culture of cranberries in the United States. The propagation, planting, cultivation, and harvesting of this American berry of folklore and tradition will satisfy anyone who is interested in a cranberry patch for the garden, providing, of course, he or she is living in a section of the country where the climate is suitable.

Send: $1.00

Ask for: "Cranberry Culture"

Write to: Redwood City Seed Co.
P.O. Box 361
Redwood City, CA 94064

Forcing Shrubs and Trees

Perhaps the most rewarding winter pleasure for gardeners is forcing flower buds of spring-blooming shrubs and trees. These buds are already formed in the fall before the onset of chilly weather. After the first of the year the buds will grow with the help of warmth and moisture. This booklet tells you what and how to cut, and how to care for branches once they're cut. Also included is a list of trees and shrubs that lend themselves to spring forcing.

Send: 35¢

Ask for: "Forcing Trees and Shrubs for Indoor Bloom"

Write to: Distribution Center C
7 Research Park
Cornell University
Ithaca, NY 14850

Just Fruit

Stark Bro's has everything a home fruit grower wants and needs. In their informative, full-color catalog they offer dwarf, semi-dwarf, and standard fruit trees including apple, peach, nectarine, cherry, pear, apricot, plum, fig, and ornamentals, and nut trees including pecan, walnut, filbert, hickory, chestnut, and butternut. You'll also find bramble fruits, grapes, strawberries, and roses. The catalog includes variety descriptions, pollination information, and planting suggestions.

Send: a postcard

Ask for: catalog

Write to: Stark Bro's Nurseries
Box B302CA
Louisiana, MO 63353

Traditional Fruits, New Varieties

This informative catalog compiled by the New York State Fruit Testing Cooperative offers hundreds of varieties of apples, peaches, plums, nectarines, and berries, often including the newest breeds available. Introduction years for all new varieties are included, as well as helpful descriptions on all the breeds offered. The cooperative will also fill orders for special requests whenever possible.

Send: donation

Ask for: "Catalog: New and Noteworthy Fruits"

Write to: New York State Fruit Testing Cooperative Association Geneva, NY 14456

Dwarf Fruit Trees

Dwarf fruit trees have several advantages over regular-size trees. They utilize sunshine better, produce better fruit, produce it earlier, and are easier to spray, prune, and harvest. If you have never raised dwarf fruit trees before, send for this little pamphlet and learn how easy it is.

Send: $1.50

Ask for: "Dwarf Fruit Trees" (No. 138J)

Write to: Consumer Information Center Dept. Z Pueblo, CO 81009

Thornless Berries

You love berries. But every pleasure has its price, and every time you go near those plants, you get hurt. If this is your story, you'll want to get acquainted with Boston Mountain Nurseries. This Arkansas-based firm specializes in *thornless* berries of all varieties.

Send: 25¢

Ask for: price list

Write to: Boston Mountain Nurseries Rt. 2 Mountainburg, AK 72946

Fruit Trees

The home gardener should consider several points very carefully before deciding to grow fruit trees. Many people become disappointed when they learn of the great care these trees require to produce quality fruit in reasonable amounts. On the other hand, home fruit growing can be a fascinating and worthwhile hobby if one is willing to devote the necessary time and effort to caring for these trees.

"Disease and Insect Control in the Home Orchard" gives you a realistic appraisal of how much and what kind of work needs to go into a prosperous orchard, so you can decide honestly whether fruit growing is for you.

Send: $1.00

Ask for: "Disease and Insect Control in the Home Orchard"

Write to: Distribution Center C
7 Research Park
Cornell University
Ithaca, NY 14850

Berries

Although they have been specializing in strawberries for over 50 years, Ahrens Strawberry Nursery carries more than strawberries. Their catalog also features tame and thornless blackberries, red and black raspberries, asparagus, three varieties of grapes, gooseberries, currants, and blueberries. Culture information for each fruit is included.

Send: a postcard

Ask for: catalog

Write to: Ahrens Strawberry Nursery
RR 1
Huntingburg, IN 47542

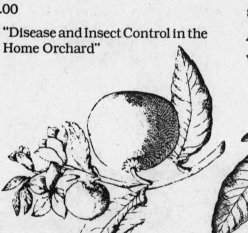

Forest Farm

Forest Farm's darling catalog comes with a list of plants, a price list, and a common-name index for gardeners not as familiar with Latin as they are with plants. Forest Farm originally sold only plants suitable for cold areas, but during the last few years they have included many unusual plants for milder climates. They carry native western plants, wild fruits, conifers, unusual ornamentals, honey plants, and dye plants. A fascinating array—difficult to find elsewhere.

Send: $1.00

Ask for: catalog

Write to: Ray and Peg Prag
Forest Farm
990 Tetherow Rd.
Williams, OR 97544

Advice for the Fruit Gardener

For the gardener considering fruit growing, or for the gardener adding a new fruit crop to an existing garden, this helpful booklet from Cornell University provides clear, intelligent information and advice. Material covered includes a discussion of soil and climatic conditions and buying tips, as well as basic instructions for preparing,

managing, and fertilizing soil. Separate chapters discuss individual fruits—tree fruits, grapes, brambles, blueberries, strawberries, currants, gooseberries, and elderberries. Also included is frank advice on eliminating destructive rodents and insects.

Send: $2.00

Ask for: "The Home Fruit Planting"

Write to: Distribution Center C
7 Research Park
Cornell University
Ithaca, NY 14850

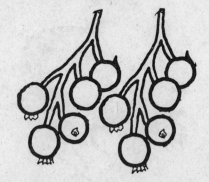

IV.
Just Flowers

Catalog of Texas Wild Flowers

This catalog specializes in seeds for Texas wild flowers and native plants. Included is information on wild flower books, cultural notes for success, poster calendars, and much, much more. The $1.00 price is refunded with a purchase of $10.00 or more.

Send: $1.00

Ask for: catalog

Write to: Green Horizons
500 Thompson Dr.
Kerrville, TX 78028

Mini-Roses

Miniature roses are a charming addition to any garden, from the most sophisticated to the rustic "natural" look. These flowers come in a great many types, they're hardy and have a profuse bloom. The catalog from Mini-Roses of Texas offers four types: bush, half-climber, trailer, and climbing, as well as new varieties and outstanding collections. Over 100 varieties are offered in all.

Send: a postcard

Ask for: rose catalog

Write to: Mini-Roses
P.O. Box 4255 Station A
Dallas, TX 75208

Beautiful Flowers for Spring and Fall

The Wayside Gardens Co. offers one of the finest nursery catalogs in the United States, and it's available for only $1.00. The fall catalog provides an array of information on fall-planted perennials and bulbs, with tips on planting. The spring catalog is considerably larger and offers listings of a wide selection of perennials, trees, shrubs, and fruit plants. Both catalogs are packed with full-color photos, an index, and an order form that makes the selection of your seeds clear and simple.

Send: $1.00

Ask for: fall catalog and/or spring catalog

Write to: The Wayside Gardens Co.
Hodges, SC 29695

Mum's the Word

If mums are your hobby, the Lehman Gardens collection is for you. Their flier features over 100 different mums, including short- and tall-stemmed varieties, and mums of every color. Blossom size ranges from "Baby Tears" with a 1″ white blossom to "Cornhusker" with a blossom of 7–8″. Lehman also offers collections to keep your garden blooming all season long, as well as special low-growing mums and mixed extra-tall varieties.

Send: a postcard

Ask for: mum price list

Write to: The Lehman Gardens
420 S.W. 10th St.
Faribault, MN 55021

American Wild Flowers

Midwest Wildflowers specializes in the plants native to the American Midwest. The catalog, illustrated with attractive line drawings, weaves facts and folklore, drawings and culture information into a captivating portrait of American wildlife. For 50¢ per package, Midwest Wildflowers carries Dutchman's breeches, jack-in-the-pulpit, wild ginger (used by the Indians for indigestion), bloodroot (good for colds and coughs), and many others.

Send: 50¢

Ask for: wild flower seed catalog or seed packages

Write to: Midwest Wildflowers
Box 64
Rockton, IL 61072

Irises

Irises are among America's favorite flower. The American Iris Society was formed for iris lovers, both professional horticulturists and amateur gardeners. AIS offers society membership and lists of specialized publications, slide programs, and iris suppliers.

Send: a postcard

Ask for: membership application and listings

Write to: The American Iris Society
6518 Beachy Ave.
Wichita, KS 67206

Alba Iris chamairis oris Ceruli.

Iris luteo Variegat

Just Roses

This catalog features roses from all over the world. Roses of Yesterday and Today specializes in roses: old, rare, unusual, and selected modern roses. Their charming catalog features black-and-white photographs of some of their selected roses, descriptions of each type, and delightful quotes pertaining to roses. Over 150 varieties.

Send: $1.50

Ask for: catalog

Write to: Roses of Yesterday and Today
802 Brown's Valley Rd.
Watsonville, CA 95076

Green Horizons

This family-run Texas business specializes in wild flowers. Their informative catalog includes books on wild flowers in the South and Southwest. In addition to culture information, and the plants themselves, they also carry wild-flower products such as note cards, calendars, and prints. Their excellent finders list suggests particular plants for specific gardening situations.

Send: $1.00 refundable on first order

Ask for: catalog

Write to: Green Horizons
500 Thompson Dr.
Kerrville, TX 78028

Begonias

Begonias are a fascinating and lovely plant. Eight major types exist, and the Thompsons offer them all. In their illustrated brochure, basic cultivation instructions are included for any environment—greenhouses, window gardens, fluorescent light gardens, terrariums, and outdoor gardens. Photographs detail the differences between groups and subgroups. Every "green thumb" will be delighted with these lush, attractive plants.

Send: $1.50

Ask for: begonia catalog

Write to: The Thompsons
310-A Hill St.
P.O. Drawer PP
Southampton, NY 11968

Magnolias

Gossler Farms Nursery specializes in magnolias. Their catalog offers much more than a description of the over 100 types of magnolia plants they carry. They offer news of the American Magnolia Society, the activities of various magnolia specialists, and an explanation of the different magnolia types. Gossler Farms keeps magnolia aficionados in touch with one another.

Send: 50¢

Ask for: magnolia catalog

Write to: Gossler Farms Nursery
1200 Weaver Rd.
Springfield, OR 97477

Wild Flowers

Clyde Robin Seed Co. specializes in wild-flower varieties. This beautiful, full-color brochure offers over 1,500 different seeds as well as garden supplies. Their offerings include Indian paint brush, poppies, lilacs, lilies, wisteria, and more exotic types. The catalog also offers some helpful planting how-tos and a bibliography. In addition, the company manages a wild-flower club and sponsors contests and special seed orders. A free package of seeds will be sent on receipt of a catalog request.

Send: $2.00

Ask for: catalog

Write to: Clyde Robin Seed Co., Inc.
P.O. Box 2855
Castro Valley, CA 94546

Flowers from Seeds

You can easily grow all annuals, biennials and many of the commonly grown herbaceous perennials from seed. This procedure requires no extensive outlay for special equipment, and it produces an abundance of plants for the home garden as well as for exchange with others who share similar gardening interests. You can derive both pleasure and satisfaction from growing your own plants from seed.

This illustrated brochure provides several useful charts and lists for the flower gardener.

Send: 35¢

Ask for: "Flowers from Seed"

Write to: Distribution Center C
7 Research Park
Cornell University
Ithaca, NY 14850

Selecting Roses

This rose-buying guide from The American Rose Society provides the ratings for the varieties of roses currently available in the United States. There is also a separate listing of the highest-rated cultivars in the various color groups, as well as detailed descriptions of the All-American Rose Selection winners. The American Rose Society is composed of a group of nearly 16,000 amateur and professional rose growers. Their booklet also contains an invitation to become a member of the society.

Send: 50¢ and a self-addressed, stamped envelope

Ask for: "Handbook for Selecting Roses"

Write to: The American Rose Society
P.O. Box 30,000
Shreveport, LA 71130

The Wilds of Missouri

From the Wilds of Missouri comes an overwhelming color catalog featuring over 600 different day lilies. Every color combination imaginable is included, and many of the flowers are photographed and reprinted in fantastic color blowups. The Wilds also offer hundreds of magnificent irises and peonies. In addition, the catalog keeps you abreast of news from the American Hemerocallis Journal and the American Peony Society. An outstandingly beautiful catalog.

Send: $2.00

Ask for: peony, iris, and day lily catalog

Write to: Gilbert H. Wild and Son, Inc.
Sarcoxie, MO 64842

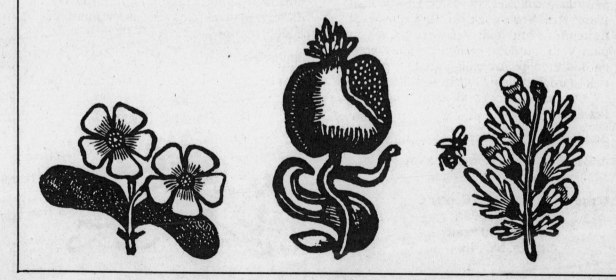

Annuals

Many varieties of annuals are colorful and easy to grow. Among the most common of these flowers are the zinnia, marigold, petunia, cornflower, and aster. This booklet from the New York State College of Agriculture and Life Sciences helps you plan your outdoor garden or start your garden indoors. An explanation of "pillow-pak" gardening is included, as well as how-to tips on cutting and exhibiting your flowers.

Send: 15¢

Ask for: "Annual Flowers for Your Garden"

Write to: Distribution Center C
7 Research Park
Cornell University
Ithaca, NY 14850

Camellias

Camellias have long been associated with romance. Orinda Nursery's catalog features large color photographs of their specialty—camellias—almost suitable for framing. The nursery also carries an assortment of rhododendrons.

Send: 50¢

Ask for: brochure

Write to: Orinda Nursery
Bridgeville, DE 19933

Miniatures

Miniature roses are natural dwarfs that are available in many of the varieties of large roses. Nor'East specializes in these perfect, tiny plants. Their color catalog provides culture information and photographs of many of the varieties available in many single- and mixed-color combinations. They also carry "Micro Minis" that are especially small, stocking nine of these tiniest plants.

Send: a postcard

Ask for: catalog

Write to: Nor'East Miniature Roses, Inc.
68 Hammond St.
Rowley, MA 01969

Dutch Tulips

Breck's bulbs come from The Hatch Garden, one of Holland's leading growers. Their beautiful color catalog features brilliant tulip mixtures, jewel hyacinths, monarchic crown imperials—an unusual spring flower with a green crown above the blossom—Grecian windflowers, snow crocuses, and many, many others. For the rarest and finest bulbs.

Send: a postcard

Ask for: catalog

Write to: Breck's
6523 N. Galena Rd.
Peoria, IL 61632

16 Tulipa purpurea Candidis oris.   17 Tulipa Carmosina.   18 Tulipa alba rubro purpureo colore saturato confusa

Wild Flowers

There was once a time when wild flowers grew feverishly in the woods. But times have changed, and there are fewer and fewer wilderness areas. Gardeners especially are aware of this loss and more and more often are growing wild flowers on their home grounds. Conley's Garden Center specializes in wild flowers. They carry bulbs, ground covers and vines, perennials, and ferns. Each plant is described in delightfully personal terms.

Roses

Jackson & Perkins offers a special catalog devoted exclusively to roses. Their roses are beautifully photographed and are available in every conceivable hue. They carry two-color tea roses, exhibition roses, Flora-tea roses grown on a shrub but with long stems, and climbers. Their color catalog also features anemones, ranunculus, gladiolus, and many other ravishing flowers.

Send: $1.00

Ask for: catalog

Write to: Conley's Garden Center
Boothbay Harbor, ME 04538

Send: a postcard

Ask for: catalog

Write to: Jackson & Perkins
Medford, OR 97501

Colorado Irises

Standard, exotic, and antique, tiny and large—these irises and day lilies from Colorado have been raised in some of nature's most ideal conditions. Good soil, plenty of Colorado sunshine, and irrigation assure the best results: big, healthy, husky, disease-free rhizomes that will grow and bloom for you.

Send: a postcard

Ask for: hardy Colorado iris and day lilies

Write to: Uranium Country Gardens
728 1675 Rd.
Delta, CO 81416

Jackson & Perkins

This Oregon company features 32 pages of bright flowers and robust vegetables. Their flower assortment includes powderpuffs, asters, chrysanthemums, candytufts, and dwarf carnations. Their bulb collection includes lilies, mums, begonias, and dahlias. More unusual items include coleus, ornamental gourds and pampas grass. They carry an equally diverse selection of vegetables.

Send: a postcard

Ask for: "Jackson & Perkins Seedbook"

Write to: Jackson & Perkins
Medford, OR 97501

Texas Wild Flowers

Want to add a touch of the Lone Star State to your garden? Here are seeds for Texas wild flowers and native plants. Take your pick: sand verbena, yarrow, century plant, lechuguilla, New Mexico agave, yellow onion, honey daisy, yellow show, blue Texas star.

Send: $1.50 each

Ask for: seed by name

Write to: Green Horizons
500 Thompson Dr.
Kerrville, TX 78028

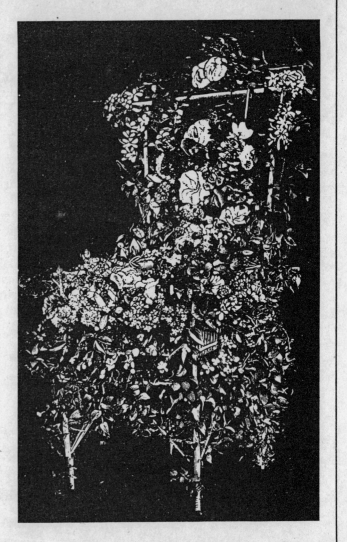

V.
Exotics

Orchid Gardens

Orchid Gardens, an organization based in Grand Rapids, sells wild flowers and hardy ferns. Their leaflet offers many varieties of woodland plants, including types of peonies, mosses, violets, and dozens of ferns. The material also includes basic cultivation advice. In addition, they run a unique slide loan library that contains nearly all their wild flowers.

Send: 50¢

Ask for: catalog

Write to: Orchid Gardens
6700 Splithand Rd.
Grand Rapids, MN 55744

Cacti and Succulents

Abbey Garden Press, associated with Abbey

Garden, the California dealer of cacti and succulents, offers dozens of books on their specialty. In addition, they carry books on regional plant studies, as well as monographs on individual genera including agave, haworthias, mammillarias, and peyote. Their catalog also contains simpler topics, such as houseplants, and specialized periodicals.

Send: free

Ask for: book catalog

Write to: Abbey Garden Press
P.O. Box 3010
Santa Barbara, CA 93105

International Gardening

Gardeners living in warm climates will go wild for the exotic fruits and vegetables available from The Banana Tree. They are specialists in rare and uncommon tropical plants. Their line includes banana types originating in Puerto Rico, Jamaica, Cuba, and India, as well as other hard-to-find fruits and vegetables such as pistachios, pomegranates, coffee, and an assortment of Chinese vegetables. For the more timid gardener, The Banana Tree also carries cold hardy trees and shrubs.

Send: a postcard

Ask for: catalog

Write to: The Banana Tree
715 Northampton St.
Easton, PA 18042

Exotic Breeds

For the adventurous gardener, Gleckler's color catalog is a must. Their offerings include flowers and vegetables from Europe and the Far East, including India and Japan. They specialize particularly in tomato breeds, but they also offer exotic items like medicinal seeds. Their catalog also includes helpful gardening hints.

Send: 50¢

Ask for: catalog

Write to: Gleckler's Seedsmen
State Rt. 120
Metamora, OH 43540

Exotic Plants

Tropical plants are exciting and exquisite. They can be grown from seeds at great savings. Many seeds from Steve Pirus come from exotic lands and are carefully chosen for their boldness and beauty. Listings include bonsais—flowering, evergreen, and deciduous; flowering vines; and novelty plants. Also included are cultural directions and reference drawings illustrating various leaf and flower shapes.

Send: 50¢

Ask for: catalog

Write to: Steve Pirus
Collector of Rare and Exotic Seeds
P.O. Box 693
Westminster, CA 92683

Orchids by Shaffer's

Considered one of the most beautiful and exotic of all flowers, the orchid holds a special fascination for many people. Shaffer's of California has been catering to orchid fanciers for 40 years. Their catalog, with price list, offers a wide range of orchids for every taste plus a list of books that will help orchid growers cultivate their beauties. A beautiful poster that will catch the eye of anyone who appreciates a thing of beauty is also included.

Send: $2.00

Ask for: catalog and poster

Write to: Shaffer's Tropical Gardens, Inc.
1220 41st Ave.
Capitola, CA 95010

Abbey Garden

The Abbey Garden cactus and succulent catalog offers outstanding photographs of these unusual species. In a clear and attractive format, these color photos depict the rich hues of desert flowers. Their selection includes not only succulents and cacti, but euphorbia, haworthia, mammillaria, and rhipsalis. The succulent enthusiast will not want to pass up this offer.

Send: $1.00

Ask for: cactus and succulent catalog

Write to: Abbey Garden
4620 Carpinteria Ave.
Carpinteria, CA 93013

Jungle Cactus

Certainly flowering cacti are among the most exceptional plants in the world. The Epiphyllum Center based in California specializes in these unusual and dramatic species. Color photographs of many of the blossoms are included. Listings are organized by size and color. Supplies, planting instructions, and a list of plant societies that particularly concern themselves with cacti and epiphyllum round out this lovely brochure.

Send: $1.00

Ask for: catalog

Write to: California EPI Center
P.O. Box 1431
Vista, CA 92083

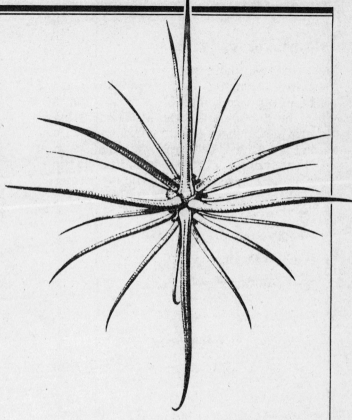

Magnificent Orchids

Many orchid species have been put on the endangered-species list. This means that they have become all the more precious. Hausermann's, a firm specializing in orchids, has begun propagating its own orchids in an effort to offset the increasing costs of imported orchids and in order to save these treasured beauties from extinction. This color catalog contains some overwhelming photographs of their stock.

Send: $1.25

Ask for: catalog

Write to: Orchids by Hausermann, Inc.
P.O. Box 363
Elmhurst, IL 60126

Carnivorous Plants

There are hundreds of types of carnivorous plants, belonging to several unrelated plant families. Carnivorous Gardens specializes in these plants, and their illustrated catalog provides a background on carnivorous species & basic cultivation information on the vast number of types. In addition to the plants themselves, the company makes available books on these unusual plants and how to grow them.

Send: $1.00

Ask for: catalog

Write to: Carnivorous Gardens
P.O. Box 331
Hamilton, NY 13346

Cacti and Succulents

For that touch of desert in your garden or for an entire desertscape, check out the succulents and cacti in Desert Dan's catalog. This is your basic, no-frills catalog—just photographs of the plants, their names, and a handy order form. A page of general instructions and growing information will get you started.

Send: $1.00

Ask for: "Illustrated Reference of Succulents and Cacti"

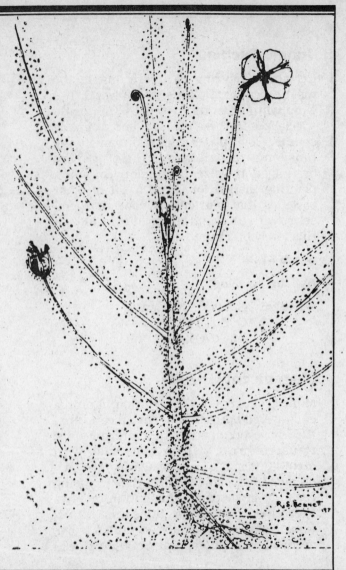

Orchids

There is something mysterious and unearthly, almost heavenly, about the lush, deep beauty of the orchid. But fashions change, even in orchids. Keep up with the latest in orchid growing with this catalog, especially if you grow orchids for competitive showing. Who knows? You may nurture a champion orchid that is uniquely different and that no one else in all the world possesses.

Send: $2.00 ($1.00 credited on first order)

Ask for: "Fennell's Orchid Jungle"

Write to: Fennell Orchid Co.
The Orchid Jungle
26715 S.W. 157th Ave.
Homestead, FL 33031

Exotica

Did you ever want to grow kiwis, persimmons, bamboo or bird of Paradise? Do you know what chicle, jojoba, and baobab are? If so, this catalog is for you. Exotica's fascinating catalog offers exotic fruits, palm trees, passion fruits, Mexican chilies, et al.

Each plant listed is accompanied by a description of its origin, its taste, and a line drawing.

Send: $2.00

Ask for: catalog

Write to: Exotica Seed Co.
8033 Sunset Blvd., Suite 125
West Hollywood, CA 90046

Lithops and Other Succulents

The increase in the cultivation of house-plants has led to a corresponding interest in succulents. These unusual and odd plants are prized by many collectors. Ed Storms offers a wide range of succulents. Everyone from the most demanding connoisseur to the novice grower will find something in this informative 22-page illustrated catalog. Soil, sun, temperature, and water requirements are discussed, and sources of further information are listed. There is also an extensive discussion of the shape, markings, and flowering patterns of each species. Many black-and-white photos illustrate shape and markings.

Send: $1.00

Ask for: "Lithops and Other Succulents"

Write to: Ed Storms, Inc.
P.O. Box 775
Azle, TX 76020

VI.
Landscaping

Famous Lawns

"Famous Lawns of America" tells you how your lawn rates against some of the finest lawns in the country. Does your lawn look as good as the one at Mount Vernon? This booklet will help it happen. Useful answers to many questions on home lawn care are included, along with photographs of these famous homes and their grounds.

Send: a postcard

Ask for: "Famous Lawns of America"

Write to: Wheel Horse
515 W. Ireland Rd.
South Bend, IN 46614

Wheel Horse

The debut edition of "Wheel Horse Magazine," a lawn and garden care magazine, is available. Wheel Horse specializes in lawn and garden equipment, especially tractors. This issue features their complete line of tractors, as well as an explanation of the mechanics of their powerful machines. Attachments may be added that allow a lawn tractor to become a snowthrower, tiller, bucket loader, small-scale bulldozer, and 3kw generator.

Send: a postcard

Ask for: "Wheel Horse Magazine"

Write to: Wheel Horse, Inc.
515 W. Ireland Rd.
South Bend, IN 46614

Landscaping Your Home

"Landscaping and Fencing" is the *Better Homes and Gardens* guide for the budget-conscious homeowner. This attractive, 50-page brochure shows you how to design your lot to complement your home. There are individual chapters on planting and maintaining your lawn, trees and shrubs, and flowers that anyone will find useful.

Many great ideas with helpful illustrations are also included on fences and screens that you can build yourself.

Send: $1.75

Ask for: C-22 "Landscaping and Fencing"

Write to: National Plan Service, Inc.
435 W. Fullerton St.
Elmhurst, IL 60126

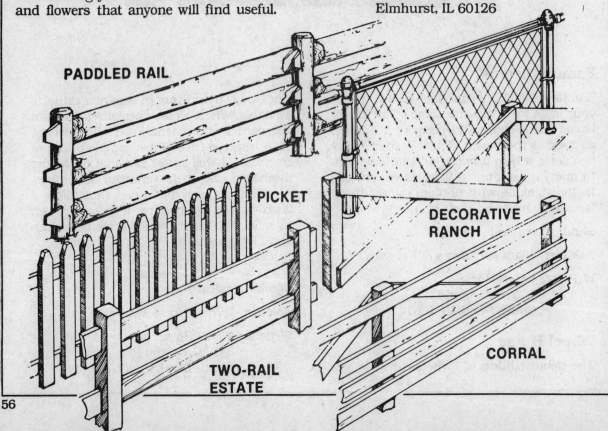

PADDLED RAIL

PICKET

DECORATIVE RANCH

TWO-RAIL ESTATE

CORRAL

Ornamental Trees and Shrubs

The "Cornell Home Garden Guide for Ornamental Trees and Shrubs" contains concise and helpful information for the gardener concerned about the care of trees and shrubs. This leaflet defines the essential terms of outdoor plant care and includes an excellent chart that tells how to plant, fertilize, mulch, prune, and water both deciduous and evergreen plants. Suggestions and illustrations on various ways to plant your shrubs are also included, as well as a list of related publications.

Send: 50¢

Ask for: "Cornell Home Garden Guide for Ornamental Trees and Shrubs" (#S112)

Write to: Distribution Center C
7 Research Park
Cornell University
Ithaca, NY 14850

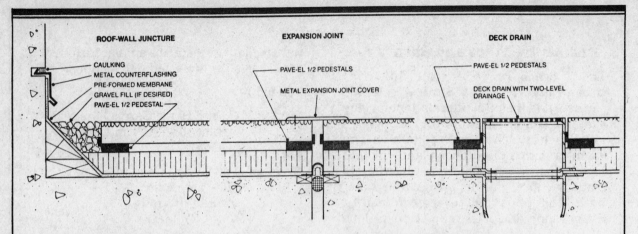

ROOF-WALL JUNCTURE

CAULKING
METAL COUNTERFLASHING
PRE-FORMED MEMBRANE
GRAVEL FILL (IF DESIRED)
PAVE-EL 1/2 PEDESTAL

EXPANSION JOINT

PAVE-EL 1/2 PEDESTALS

METAL EXPANSION JOINT COVER

DECK DRAIN

PAVE-EL 1/2 PEDESTALS

DECK DRAIN WITH TWO-LEVEL
DRAINAGE

Outdoor Decks

Pave-El is a pedestal system for outdoor decks designed to meet North American climatic and architectural requirements. Precast paving slabs, set into a sand or gravel bed, the conventional method, are subject to deterioration due to weather-related stress. Pave-El leveling plates may be stacked, aligning one paved surface with another. Strong, sturdy, and self-cleaning, Pave-El squares deserve the attention of homeowners and gardeners.

Send: a postcard

Ask for: brochure

Write to: Envirospec, Inc.
Ellicott Station
P.O. Box 119
Buffalo, NY 14205

A Natural Landscape

Vick's Wildgardens offers nearly 100 wild flowers and plants to create a unique natural landscape around your home. Their catalog includes drawings of every plant they sell, as well as culture instructions for the wild-flower gardener. Located in Gladwyne, Pennsylvania, they also offer a landscape service to those in their area.

Send: 50¢

Ask for: wild flower and fern catalog

Write to: Vick's Wildgardens, Inc.
Conshohocken State Rd., below
Spring Mill Rd.
Box 115
Gladwyne, PA 19035

Lawns

The Better Lawn and Turf Institute offers concise scientific advice for lawn growers in all regions of America. "Lawns and Their Tending" offers a comparative overview of available lawn grasses and useful information on preparation, seeding, and maintenance. Practical hints are also provided on controlling weeds and insects.

Send: a self-addressed, stamped envelope

Ask for: "Lawns and Their Tending"

Write to: The Lawn Institute
991 W. 5th St.
Marysville, OH 43040

Lilypons

Lilypons carries everything necessary for constructing and maintaining your own goldfish pond. Their water lilies are truly spectacular, including especially fragrant types, lilies that change color, day- and night-blooming types, annuals, and hardy perennials. They also carry lotus plants (the sacred Far Eastern flower), many different goldfish, accessory and oxygenating plants to ensure the health of your goldfish, and everything you'll need for pond maintenance. The catalog itself contains magnificent photographs of their lilies and private lily gardens, as well as helpful articles on planting and winter care, and protecting the health of your fish.

Send: $2.00

Ask for: catalog

Write to: Lilypons Water Gardens
Lilypons, MD 21717
or
Brookshire, TX 77423

Ground Covers

Spectacular, thick ground huggers are featured in Spring Hill's color catalog. Ground covers include "Blue Rug Juniper" pachysandra, hypericum, golden sedum, and Irish moss. Flowers include old favorites like the bleeding heart and forget-me-nots. More unusual flowering plants such as Chinese lanterns, baby's breath, and sea lavender are also available.

Landscaping Around the House

Every homeowner wants to have an attractive lot around the house. How to do it? Don't just start planting trees and shrubs! Learn the fine art of landscaping and turn the yard and garden around your home into an aesthetically pleasing vista to the delight of your friends and neighbors. This pamphlet will give you the help to plan your yard carefully.

Send: a postcard

Ask for: "Planting Book"

Write to: Spring Hill Nurseries
Reservation Center
Dept. 6523
N. Galena Rd.
Peoria, IL 61632

Send: a postcard

Ask for: "Landscaping Around the Home—Get Help, Plan Carefully" (No. 556J)

Write to: Consumer Information Center
Dept. Z
Pueblo, CO 81009

Water, Rocks, and Sculpture

Here are some garden secrets to make your garden more exotic and picturesque. A do-it-yourself project employing rocks, pools, waterfalls, stone planters, and sculpture can enhance the physical beauty of any garden. This rocklike material can be sawed, chipped, drilled, and carved so that you can meet the unique requirements of your garden. Write for this leaflet and learn more about "featherock."

Send: 25¢

Ask for: "Featherock Garden Secrets"

Write to: Featherock, Inc.
2890 Empire St.
Burbank, CA 91510

Ornamental Grasses

At least 80 kinds of ornamental grasses are suitable for garden use and they require minimal maintenance. "Ornamental Grasses for the Home and Garden" was written by faculty members at the New York State College of Agriculture and Life Sciences at Cornell University. This illustrated brochure includes a key to various grasses, a glossary of terms, and culture and maintenance instructions. In addition, suggestions are provided for using ornamental grasses in dried arrangements, and lists of further reading and reference material and suppliers are included.

Send: 30¢

Ask for: "Ornamental Grasses for the Home and Garden"

Write to: Distribution Center C
7 Research Park
Cornell University
Ithaca, NY 14850

Send: $2.00

Ask for: "Water Visions"

Write to: Van Ness Water Gardens
2460 N. Euclid
Upland, CA 91786

Water Gardens

Water in the garden brings refreshing cool on the hottest summer day. It is calming, beautifying, satisfying to the eye. In it the clouds and sky are gently reflected. Water can also give your garden a touch of the tropics, the Orient, the rural countryside. Learn what water can do for your garden with this handsome brochure that shows you what is on the market and gives you how-to tips as well.

Lawn Care

"Lawn Care" is devoted to the care and improvement of home lawns. Each issue of this colorful publication includes a seasonal checklist to remind you what needs to be done when, a page of reader questions, and specific articles on solving lawn problems and recent developments in the field. "Lawn Care" also includes garden tips. This magazine should be on every serious homeowner's reading list.

Send: a postcard

Ask for: "Lawn Care"

Write to: Scotts
Marysville, OH 43041

Beautify Your Home

Beautiful homes are the dream of many people, but many homeowners never get beyond the dream because they think that landscaping their yards and grounds will be too expensive. In some cases, they just don't know where to begin. Learn how to plant and organize the ground area around your house with this pamphlet that will make your yard both useful and attractive.

Send: a self-addressed, stamped envelope

Ask for: "Home Beautification"

Write to: Information Officer
West Virginia Dept. of Agriculture
Capitol Building
Charleston, WV 25305

New Breeds of Lawn Grasses

The Lawn Institute reviews and reports on new lawn-grass cultivars. They are looking for grasses that show disease tolerance, an attractive weed-free texture, and decumbent growth. Their "update" includes a comparative survey of Kentucky bluegrasses, perennial ryes, fine fescues, and specialty grasses to provide you with all the current scientific information you need for today's fine lawn.

Send: a self-addressed, stamped envelope

Ask for: "Lawn Cultivar Update"

Write to: The Lawn Institute
991 W. 5th St.
Marysville, OH 43040

VII.
Gardening Techniques:
Composting, Soil Improvement, Weed Management

Weeds

What is a weed? This little pamphlet will tell you, and, what's more, it will tell you what to do about them. The basic weed groupings are defined and the basic remedies for controlling and preventing weeds are detailed. Since scattered weeds will appear occasionally even in the best-cared-for lawns, know what to do before and after they arrive.

Send: a postcard

Ask for: "Weeds?"

Write to: Consumer Affairs Department
Chevron Chemical Co.
P.O. Box 3744
San Fransisco, CA 94119

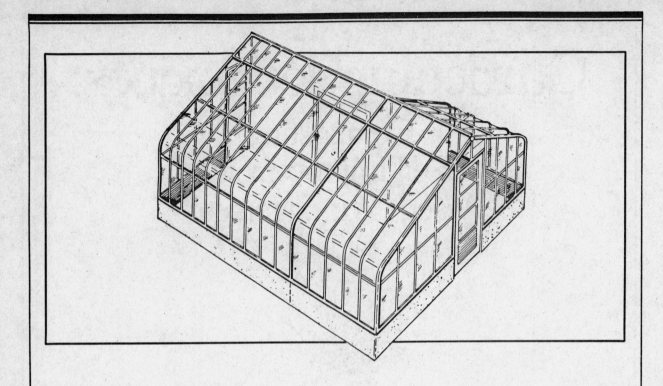

Living Walls

Living Wall gardens require no arable land, will grow in both warm and chilly climates, and are simple to assemble. What are Living Walls? They are fiberglass containers in which your plants can flourish in well-ordered planting spaces. It includes a simple irrigation system and a time-controlled fertilization system. The color brochure tells all.

Send: a postcard

Ask for: brochure

Write to: Living Wall Garden Co.
RD #3
Naples, NY 14512

Raised-Bed Gardening

Raised-bed gardening can improve your produce yield dramatically. By companion planting, interplanting, and succession planting, plants stay healthier since the soil is more conducive to plant development. This instructive manual details the how-tos of these various techniques and lets you in on the secret of making soil work for you.

More on Weeds

Weeds, or any plants growing where they're not wanted, are a nuisance. Learning to identify them and knowing the best way to uproot them ensures your garden the nutrients of the soil and the light of the sun. "Weeds in Ornamental Plantings," a 14-page booklet from the New York State College of Agriculture and Life Sciences, identifies those weeds for you and tells you how to get rid of them.

Send: $1.25

Ask for: "How to Maximize Garden Yields with Raised Beds"

Write to: Butterbrooke Farm
78 Barry Rd.
Oxford, CT 06483

Send: 50¢

Ask for: "Weeds in Ornamental Plantings"

Write to: Distribution Center C
Research Park
Cornell University
Ithaca, NY 14850

Garden Chemicals

As every gardener knows, the various chemicals used in tending a garden can be dangerous. Here is a colorful chart that gives you safety tips on mixing and applying, storing, disposal, spills, and first-aid treatment for those mishaps that are bound to occur sooner or later. Learn these commonsense rules and plant a safer garden!

Send: a postcard

Ask for: "Garden Chemicals and Common Sense"

Write to: Consumer Affairs Department
Chevron Chemical Co.
P.O. Box 3744
San Francisco, CA 94119

Guide to Scientific Composting

Composting is an essential element of the current trend in organic gardening. A handy seven-page booklet called "Guide to Scientific Composting" describes the how and why of composting. There is also a breakdown of the function of the microorganisms that are vital to the formation of humus.

Send: 25¢

Ask for: "Guide to Scientific Composting"

Write to: Ringer Corporation
Dept. P81
6860 Flying Cloud Dr.
Eden Prairie, MN 55344

Judd Ringer's Catalog

Judd Ringer's 16-page catalog is a valuable source for organic gardeners—or for any gardeners interested in improving the health and quality of their plants. Tree and shrub boosters, tomato grow rings, lawn restorers, and soil builders are listed along with brief explanations on how to use the products and the effects they will have on your garden. Diagrams are included.

Send: 25¢

Ask for: Judd Ringer's organic garden product catalog

Write to: Ringer Research
Dept. P81
6860 Flying Cloud Dr.
Eden Prairie, MN 55344

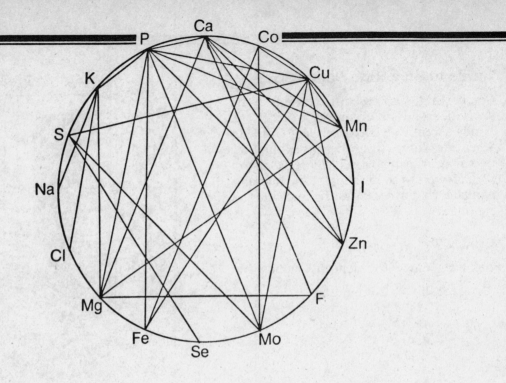

Give Your Plants the Best

You can have bigger crops than ever! The secret is in the soil. Rich soil has all the nutrients essential to healthy plant growth. Sudbury offers soil test kits to assess the shortcomings of your soil. They also carry soil additives, seed starters, and animal repellents, all featured in their color brochure. For the finest flowers and vegetables you've ever seen, start with fine soil.

Send: a postcard

Ask for: "The Secret in the Soil" catalog

Write to: Sudbury Laboratory, Inc.
572 Dutton Rd.
Sudbury, MA 01776

Weeds

Weeds have a terrible reputation. This 16-page booklet tries to dispel some of these myths. There are 45 different weeds presented, all with descriptions, photographs, and suggestions on how to find them and how to use them. Many of the varieties featured are flowering types and are just as beautiful as many conventional garden flowers. A list of additional sources is also included.

Send: 25¢

Ask for: "Weeds"

Write to: Distribution Center C
7 Research Park
Cornell University
Ithaca, NY 14850

Companion Planting

Companion planting makes good common sense. The "Primer of Companion Planting" details for both the novice and experienced gardener the benefits of herb gardening. Companion planting with herbs exploits nature's assets in protecting your garden from insects, and enriching the soil for your fruits, vegetables, and flowers. This booklet offers the most recent scientific information on plant and animal interaction.

Send: $1.50

Ask for: "Primer of Companion Planting"

Write to: The Bio-Dynamic Farming and Gardening Association, Inc.
P.O. Box 253
Wyoming, RI 02898

Earthworms

Every gardener should know about earthworms. This book will tell you about the various types of earthworms and the beneficial things they do for the soil. What are their effects on moisture, air, and the nutrients of your garden's soil? How significant is their influence on crop yield? Do you need to introduce earthworms into your garden? Earthworms make the difference…spindly grass or lush growth?

Send: $2.00

Ask for: "What Every Gardener Should Know About Earthworms" (Garden Way Bulletin A-21)

Write to: Garden Way Publishing
Dept. A979
Charlotte, VT 05445

Weeds Used in Medicine

As the state of the medicinal art has advanced by leaps and bounds since this 1904 government publication on useful weeds first came out, the information contained in it has only antiquarian value. But for anyone interested in how early 20th-century farmers could have turned patches of weeds into profits and what weeds contain health-restoring properties, this little booklet is quaint and interesting. For example, if your yard was overrun with a weed called Blessed Thistle, you could cultivate it and export it to Germany at about 8¢ to 10¢ per pound. Alas, it's no longer 1904!

Send: $2.00

Ask for: "Weeds Used in Medicine"

Write to: Redwood City Seed Co.
P.O. Box 361
Redwood City, CA 94064

Soil Improvement

Soil is not just dirt. It's the bed in which your garden grows. Sometimes it needs improvement. This book will tell you about soil conditioners, insects, water, drainage, nutrients, diseases, and when is the best time to improve your soil. The topsoil in your garden may need a little help and encouragement from you. Here are practical things to do, explained step by step with diagrams and illustrations to make it easy.

Send: $2.00

Ask for: "Improving Your Soil" (Garden Way Bulletin A-20)

Write to: Garden Way Publishing
Dept. A979
Charlotte, VT 05445

Necessary Trading

Necessary Trading Co.'s purpose is to provide complete service for biological agriculture to amateur gardeners and large commercial farms. Their intelligent and informative catalog explains the benefits of biological fertilizers and discusses the different types. Their services also include composting supplies, five different soil tests, and foliar nutrients. The chapter on foliars contains excellent tips on how to feed different plants. A must for the ecologically aware gardener.

Send: $1.50

Ask for: biological farming catalog

Write to: Necessary Trading Co.
New Castle, VA 24127

Compost—What It Is

This 18-page booklet is a thorough and detailed study for the gardener considering compost. Topics include compost makeup and types, its use, sanitation and flies, and an explanation of the process of decomposition. The organic gardener could not find a more complete discussion of this issue. A handy reference manual. An extra 50¢ postage and handling fee is required.

Send: $2.00

Ask for: "Compost"

Write to: The Bio-Dynamic Farming and
          Gardening Association, Inc.
          P.O. Box 253
          Wyoming, RI 02898

Seaweed

Seaweed is a natural mineral supplement for plants and for the soil. It includes essential trace elements for your plants—zinc, copper, and manganese. Seaweed has been reported to increase cold resistance, yields, sugar content, and germination. The results of these studies are available from Maxicrop, a distributor of a seaweed-based plant food.

Send: a postcard

Ask for: Maxicrop brochure

Write to: Maxicrop, U.S.A., Inc.
          P.O. Box 964
          Arlington Heights, IL 60006

Soil Conditioners

For samples of organic soil conditioners and fertilizers, write to Fertility Acres and receive yours by mail. Types include: greensand, soft rock phosphate, granite dust, cottonseed meal, bone meal, blood meal, and diatomaceous earth. You can also write for a free catalog.

Send: a #10, self-addressed, stamped envelope for catalog or $2.00 for samples

Write to: Fertility Acres, Inc.
P.O. Box 249
West Newton, PA 15089

VIII.
Tools and Accessories

Garden Furniture

The elegance and grace of old southern outdoor furniture is captured by Moultrie's reproductions in cast aluminum. Their catalog offers the sophisticated filigree of southern living in plant stands, fountains, breakfast and dining sets, mailboxes, and many other charming ideas that enhance every home and garden.

Send: $1.00

Ask for: catalog

Write to: Moultrie Manufacturing Co.
P.O. Drawer 1179
Moultrie, GA 31768

Tools Dependent on Human Energy

Want to know the best way to mow hay, cut weeds, split firewood, or harvest small grains? By Hand & Foot, Ltd., has researched every tool for these tasks and found the most effective tools available. In two brochures, they show you which tools enhance rather than abuse your body, and thus make simple tasks more enjoyable. They even have some tools that are made especially for children to use safely and effectively. Each brochure is fully illustrated, and includes an order form for easy shopping.

Send: $1.00

Ask for: "Mowing Hay, Cutting Weeds, and Harvesting Small Grains with the Scythe"
"The Best Way to Split Firewood"

Write to: By Hand & Foot, Ltd.
P.O. Box 611
Brattleboro, VT 05301

Garden Talk

Walt Nicke's "Garden Talk" catalog is filled with a unique selection of inexpensive items perfect for the amateur or professional gardener. Here you will find English thatched-roof birdhouses, snail bait holders, plastic flowerpots that can be steam-sterilized, a 3½" pocket-size pruner, and much, much more. Walt suggests you take your time and read it all slowly.

Send: 50¢

Ask for: "Garden Talk"

Write to: Walter F. Nicke
Box 667G
Hudson, NY 12534

Tools, Tools, Tools

A. M. Leonard's hefty horticultural tool and supply catalog is a 75-page, lavishly illustrated compendium of information and supplies for the gardener. They offer *everything* for the gardener and the lover of the great outdoors. Leonard carries power and manual tools, fertilizers, pesticides, measuring tapes, oilstones, clothing, safety equipment, reference books, and much more.

Send: a postcard

Ask for: tool catalog

Write to: A. M. Leonard, Inc.
6665 Spiker Rd.
Piqua, OH 54356

Garden Accessories

Gardens are more than just the flowers and plants that grow in them. This colorful catalog from Gardener's Eden will show you many accessories for decorative and maintenance purposes that you may need to improve your present garden or for a garden you would like to create. See what's available in a wide price range.

Send: $1.00

Ask for: catalog

Write to: Gardener's Eden
25 Huntington at Copley Square
Boston, MA 02116

Gardening Tools

Veteran gardeners know about Smith & Hawken. They import fine garden implements from an English manufacturer carrying such standards as forks, spades, and watering cans, as well as more unusual items including snaths, scythes, and children's tools. Their lovely, illustrated, 30-page brochure offers the history of the company, and an explanation of fine tool construction.

Send: $1.00

Ask for: tool catalog

Write to: Smith & Hawken, Ltd.
Dept. 092
68 Homer
Palo Alto, CA 94301

Violet House

This Florida plant dealer sells plant products by mail. The catalog includes flowerpots in various sizes and shapes, water reservoirs, and hanging baskets. They also carry specialized fertilizers, limestone, peat moss, fish emulsion, and insect sprays.

Send: a postcard

Ask for: "Catalog on Pots, Hanging Baskets, Fertilizers, and Plant Materials"

Write to: The Violet House
P.O. Box 1274
15 S.E. 4th Ave.
Gainesville, FL 32601

Tools for Country Living

Eventually almost every gardener learns to preserve his good fruits and vegetables. Countryside General provides the tools needed for bottling and canning those delicious fresh foods. They also offer books on herb and vegetable gardening as well as other aspects of country life.

Send: $1.00

Ask for: catalog

Write to: Countryside General
Hwy. 19 East
Waterloo, WI 53594

IX.
Insects
and
Disease

Vegetables: Insect and Disease Control

Knowing how to recognize and control some of the most common pests that plague vegetable gardens can greatly increase your yield. This booklet tells you how to use insecticide and fungicide safely, and also discusses which pests prey on specific vegetables. Clever drawings illustrate how to use pesticide equipment, and a list of precautions is included. In addition, photographs of most of the common vegetable predators make identification simple.

Send: $1.25

Ask for: "Insect and Disease Control on Vegetables"

Write to: Distribution Center C
7 Research Park
Cornell University
Ithaca, NY 14850

Beneficial Insects

Work with nature, not against her! This is the philosophy of gardeners who would let beneficial insects do the job of suppressing pests to more tolerable levels. This safe, effective, low-cost method is now available, and you can learn about it free by writing for this manual on pest-management programs. Remember: Pests are only pests when they occur in intolerable numbers. So use biological control to reduce those numbers in your garden.

Send: a postcard

Ask for: pest-management brochure

Write to: Rincon-Vitova Insectaries
P.O. Box 95
Oak View, CA 93022

Dying Trees

This booklet focuses on what happens when a tree decays and eventually dies. The full-color drawings in this 28-page booklet give an accurate presentation of tree decay, showing the major stages of an extremely complex process involving interaction among the deadly microorganisms, environmental factors, and the tree itself. A fascinating and informative way to learn about the largest and sometimes oldest living plants on earth.

Send: $1.30

Ask for: "A Tree Hurts, Too"

Write to: U.S. Government Printing Office
Superintendent of Documents
Washington, DC 20402

Protecting Your Vegetable Garden

Disease and insects can damage your vegetable crop from the time seeds are planted until after the crops are picked. This illustrated bulletin recommends certain basic steps (outlined in an easy-to-read chart) to be followed each year for controlling the most destructive pests that prey on garden vegetables. Included are discussions of plant diseases and destructive insects, and the pros and cons of chemical insecticides, fungicides, soil treatments, and seed treatments. A must for the gardeners who want the most from their gardens.

Send: $1.00

Ask for: "Insects and Diseases in the Home Vegetable Garden"

Write to: Distribution Center C
7 Research Park
Cornell University
Ithaca, NY 14850

Fungicides and Pesticides

The use of chemicals in soil management is a highly controversial topic. This report, written by an agricultural research professor, is an intelligent discussion of this volatile and crucial subject. The soil's role in maintaining the earth's ecology is given special emphasis. This pamphlet makes worthwhile reading for every gardener.

Send: 85¢

Ask for: "The Living Soil Protects Plants"

Write to: The Bio-Dynamic Farming and
Gardening Association, Inc.
P.O. Box 253
Wyoming, RI 02898

Natural Control of Garden Pests

An essential part of organic gardening is learning to safeguard your plants without pesticides. These handout sheets offer over a dozen natural ways of keeping destructive pests out of your garden. Geraniums keep out most insects. Marigolds protect tomatoes. A list of other useful insect-deterring plants is available from the Urban Gardening Program in Philadelphia.

Send: a postcard

Ask for: "Organic Gardening" handout sheets

Write to: Urban Gardening Program
Pennsylvania State University
S.E. corner Broad and Grange Sts.
Philadelphia, PA 19141

Garden Pests

The Urban Gardening Program will send you four brochures on garden pests: cabbage insects, the Mexican bean beetle, the Japanese beetle, and aphids. These illustrated brochures suggest natural prevention methods, recommended amounts of pesticide application, and precautions on pesticide use. Also offered are individual information sheets on

various destructive insects. Each sheet describes the insect's life cycle, the vegetables in which each burrows, and antidotes. The insect sheets available are: cabbage worm, aphids, whitefly, squash vine borer, squash bug, spider mites, spotted and striped cucumber beetle, slugs, maggots, nematodes, bean beetle, leafhoppers, hornworm, cutworm, corn borer, and potato beetle.

Send: a postcard

Ask for: garden pest brochures and individual insect sheets

Write to: Urban Gardening Program
Pennsylvania State University
S.E. corner Broad and Grange Sts.
Philadelphia, PA 19141

Pest Control

Wherever vegetables are raised—large farm, small backyard plot—they are vulnerable to the ravages of insect pests and plant diseases. Much loss can be avoided at a very nominal cost to the grower by using timely remedies and practicing good cultural and sanitation methods. But it requires work and planning. So before you plant, check out this handy pamphlet for ways to make your vegetable garden a safe environment for your produce.

Send: self-addressed, stamped envelope

Ask for: "Home Vegetable Garden Pest Control"

Write to: Information Officer
West Virginia Dept. of Agriculture
Capitol Building
Charleston, WV 25305

Pest-Proofing Your Garden

Two things will probably determine your methods of ridding your garden of pests: the type of pest and your philosophy of extermination. If you are against killing living creatures, you will have to find other ways than the shotgun or lethal poisons. On the other hand, death might be the solution you reserve for some pests like mice and squirrels, but not rabbits and deer. Whatever kind of rascal is tormenting your garden, learn alternative ways of saying "Scat!"

Send: $2.00

Ask for: "Scat! Pest-Proofing Your Garden" (Garden Way Bulletin A-15)

Write to: Garden Way Publishing
Dept. A979
Charlotte, VT 05445

X.
Indoor Gardening

Houseplants

This 32-page book from the U.S. Dept. of Agriculture will give you all the information you need for selecting and growing houseplants. Plants are listed alphabetically by types. General instructions cover humidity, watering, potting, fertilizing, summer care, and growing your plants by dim light.

Send: $1.75

Ask for: "Selecting and Growing House Plants" (Home and Garden Bulletin 139J)

Write to: Consumer Information Center
Dept. Z
Pueblo, CO 81009

African Violets Their Specialty

For just 50¢, Fischer Greenhouses will send you their 16-page, full-color African violet catalog, their 32-page indoor garden supply catalog, plus a helpful eight-page brochure filled with tips on how to raise African violets. An offer not to be missed.

Send: 50¢

Ask for: catalogs

Write to: Fischer Greenhouses
Oak Ave., Dept. FT
Linwood, NJ 08221

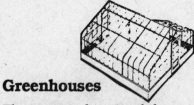

Greenhouses

The many architectural shapes and designs of modern greenhouses are clearly illustrated by photograph and blueprint in this catalog. Also included are accessories such as heaters and coolers, nozzles, vents, and benches. The finest in aluminum greenhouses.

Send: a postcard

Ask for: catalog

Write to: Aluminum Greenhouses, Inc.
14605 Lorain Ave.
Cleveland, OH 44111

Cold Frames

With a cold frame you can stretch your short growing season for vegetables up to three months in some areas. What is a cold frame? A simple box of boards set on the ground outdoors and topped with a secondhand storm window. Learn how to make and use a cold frame with this instructional manual. Think of how proud you'll be to serve Thanksgiving dinner with a salad from your own cold garden!

Send: $2.00

Ask for: "Building and Using Cold Frames" (Garden Way Bulletin A-39)

Write to: Garden Way Publishing
Dept. A979
Charlotte, VT 05445

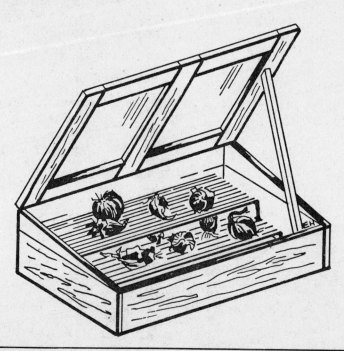

Plants

Lauray of Salisbury has a catalog of plants that can be ordered by mail from their nursery in Connecticut. Gesneriads, begonias, succulents, cacti, orchids, and other houseplants are listed in this straightforward shipping catalog.

Send: $1.25

Ask for: catalog

Write to: Lauray of Salisbury
Undermountain Rd.
Rt. 41
Salisbury, CT 06068

Indoor Gardener

Grower's Supply Co. provides the essentials for the indoor gardener. Their fliers offer plant trays, greenhouses, fluorescent light fixtures, timers, suitable for any arrangement. Attractive and space-saving, all you need to do is supply the plants.

Send: a postcard

Ask for: flier and price list

Write to: Grower's Supply Co.
P.O. Box 1132
33 N. Staebler
Ann Arbor, MI 48106

Gothic Greenhouses

Greenhouses need not be expensive investments. An economical, sunny, energy-efficient greenhouse may be sensibly purchased by taking advantage of tax credits and your own labor. Gothic Arch shows you how. Their color brochure discusses irrigation and heating/cooling options, and their kits include everything you need to start building. "A Practical Guide to Greenhouse Selection" also answers many questions for the prospective buyer.

Send: a postcard

Ask for: catalog

Write to: Gothic Arch Greenhouses
P.O. Box 1564
Mobile, AL 36633

Tropical Plants

Send for this free brochure and price list of accessories for your tropical plants. Full-color photographs show you in detail how you can enhance your tropical greenery with hand-carved pots and hanging baskets. Also available are slabs and totems made out of fibers and barks and hand-carved into interesting totem and animal shapes.

Send: a self-addressed, stamped envelope

Ask for: catalog

Write to: Tropical Plant Products
1715 Silver Star Rd.
P.O. Box 7754
Orlando, FL 32804

Cold-Frame Plans

Want to make your own cold frame for growing vegetables long beyond the official growing season? Write to Dalen Products for a free set of cold-frame plans that detail the construction of a 3′-by-6′ automatic cold frame built from a single (4′-by-8′) sheet of plywood.

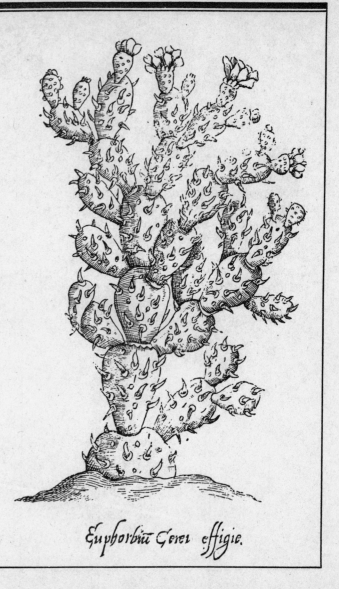

Euphorbia Cerei effigie.

Send: a postcard

Ask for: cold-frame plans

Write to: Customer Services
Dalen Products
201 Serlake Dr.
Knoxville, TN 37922

Bromeliads

This 44-page catalog of bromeliads and selected exotics includes an extensive horticultural book listing and a complete line of supplies necessary to home bromeliad care, a glossary, and an information source list. Discount coupons will also be sent along with this catalog.

Send: a postcard

Ask for: "Tropiflora Bromeliads"

Write to: Tropiflora
5439 3rd St. East
Bradenton, FL 33507

Poisonous Household Plants

In recent years, more and more people have been using plants for interior decoration in both homes and offices. Are some of these seemingly innocuous plants dangerous if ingested? This pamphlet will explain the various precautions you should take if you have a child who is in the habit of eating household plants. Learn which plants should be avoided and what remedies to take should your children ingest a toxic plant.

Send: a self-addressed, stamped envelope

Ask for: "Houseplants—How Poisonous Are They?"

Write to: Information Officer
West Virginia Dept. of Agriculture
Capitol Building
Charleston, WV 25305

Terrariums

An English botanist is credited with developing the first terrarium, an environment that would protect plants from drying out and enable young plants to grow under perfectly controlled conditions. In the modern home terrariums have been found to bring a delightful decorative touch to any room. "How to Make a Terrarium" from the New York State College of Agriculture and Life Sciences tells you what kind of containers to use and what type of plants are most appropriate to terrarium living, and details the planting and maintenance procedure.

Send: 15¢

Ask for: "How to Make a Terrarium"

Write to: Distribution Center C
7 Research Park
Cornell University
Ithaca, NY 14850

It Runs on the Sun and Not Much Else

Gardeners have always known that greenhouses make efficient use of the sun's energy to aid the growth of their plants. Now the Vegetable Factory brings you a greenhouse that will help you utilize the sun's rays in other ways as well. Their attractive 16-page, full-color brochure describes the advantages of their solar-panel greenhouse. The brochure also includes a question-and-answer section, a discussion of the tax credits available to homeowners who install greenhouses, a comparative heating cost table, and a listing of all currently available greenhouse models.

Send: $2.00

Ask for: greenhouse catalog

Write to: Vegetable Factory, Inc.
Dept P-111
P.O. Box 2235
New York, NY 10163

Houseplants and Their Environment

Most people select their houseplants by appearance. They know they want something red or leafy or hanging or bushy. How often have you chosen your plants this way and then watched them die in a matter of weeks or days? This pamphlet will explain the basic principles of houseplants and their environmental needs. Light, water, humidity, fertilizer, soil, plant food, temperature, insects—these factors and more should be taken into consideration by every indoor plant enthusiast.

Send: a self-addressed, stamped envelope

Ask for: "Houseplants, An Environmental View"

Write to: Information Officer
West Virginia Dept. of Agriculture
Capitol Building
Charleston, WV 25305

Rare Plants

For 21 years Kartuz Greenhouses has been supplying flower lovers with rare and

unusual plants. Their catalog features the leading hybridizers of indoor plants. If you are interested in gesneriads, begonias, or other plants, send for this colorful 24-page catalog and inspect them for yourself.

Send: $1.00

Ask for: catalog

Write to: Kartuz Greenhouses
1408 Sunset Dr.
Vista, CA 92083

Houseplants of the Future

The old standbys like philodendrons, spider plants, and piggybacks may be getting you down. If so, look into these tropical plants that will grow equally well in your home, apartment, or patio. They are called bromeliads and flower only once, but offshoots can be harvested. Ask for this free one-page explanation of this exotic plant and you may be converted.

Send: a postcard

Ask for: "Houseplants of the Future"

Write to: Shelldance
2000 Cabrillo Hwy.
Pacifica, CA 94044

Indoor Gardens

This flier is great for the beginning gardener. Full of suggestions and simple household ideas on caring for your plants, it also contains lists of common foliage and flowering plants, and a list of the light required for some of the most popular houseplants. In addition, the process of plant growth and photosynthesis is explained.

Send: free to New York State residents; 15¢ elsewhere

Ask for: "Indoor Gardening"

Write to: Distribution Center C
7 Research Park
Cornell University
Ithaca, NY 14850

Carnivorous and Woodland Terrarium Plants

You can order everything you need to begin a woodland or carnivorous plant terrarium. Many of the plant listings are accompanied by black-and-white photographs. Also included are line drawings detailing the leaf shapes of some of the plant types. This four-page flier offers greenhouse containers and accessories as well as a selection of books to help you pursue your hobby.

Send: a self-addressed, stamped envelope

Ask for: carnivorous plant catalog

Write to: Peter Pauls Nurseries
Canandaigua, NY 14424

Container Gardening

Container gardening means more produce from less space. For the urban gardener this method is essential. A surprising number of vegetables can be grown indoors in simple containers. Carrots, lettuce, onions, and spinach all grow well indoors. Containers may be constructed from old tires, cement blocks, buckets, and crates. These handout sheets offer many clever ideas for the city dweller. Advice on soil mixture, planting, and hydroponic gardening is included.

Send: a postcard

Ask for: "Container Gardening" handout sheets

Write to: Urban Gardening Program
Pennsylvania State University
S.E. corner Broad and Grange Sts.
Philadelphia, PA 19141

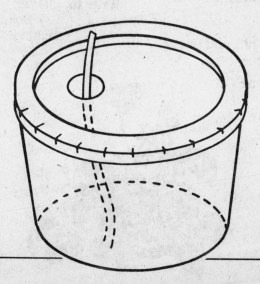

Indoor Flowering Plants

Plants and flowers bring nature's beauty indoors. Contemporary use of plants ranges from extensive plantings in urban shopping areas to displays in today's homes and apartments with large expanses of glass. This 30-page booklet offers information on growth requirements, a listing of specific flowering plants, and a listing of popular houseplants and their light requirements. Also included is a chapter on decorative uses—how to select complementary plants, how to choose attractive containers, etc.

Send: 75¢

Ask for: "The Selection, Care, and Use of Plants in the Home"

Write to: Distribution Center C
7 Research Park
Cornell University
Ithaca, NY 14850

Do-It-Yourself Planter

You can make a simple and attractive planter from nearly any three- to five-gallon plastic container. Planter of Texas tells you how. In these easy-to-understand conversion and assembly instructions, each step is delineated and accompanied by an illustration. A great idea for the self-sufficient indoor gardener.

Send: $2.00

Ask for: "Planter Plans"

Write to: Planter
P.O. Box 5238
Temple, TX 76501

Indoor Gardening

For the gardener with limited space or living in the city, indoor gardening is often the only course. Fortunately, a few garden suppliers cater especially to those needs. Indoor Gardening Supplies offers you a great variety of window racks, plant shelves, indoor greenhouses, fluorescent fixtures, soil analyzers, and humidifiers in an attractive, illustrated brochure. Everything you need for a self-sufficient indoor garden.

Send: a postcard

Ask for: catalog

Write to: Indoor Gardening Supplies
P.O. Box 40567F
Detroit, MI 48240

Plant Cuttings

Plant cuttings are a fun way of propagating your houseplants, and they are a perfect project for young gardeners. This flier from the New York State College of Agriculture and Life Sciences tells you everything you'll need and how to go about cutting and replanting your favorite plants. Five different types of cuttings are outlined, with diagrams illustrating each one.

Send: free to residents of New York State; 15¢ elsewhere

Ask for: "Growing House Plants from Cuttings"

Write to: Distribution Center C
7 Research Park
Cornell University
Ithaca, NY 14850

Houseplants

This handy manual for houseplants edited by *Better Homes and Gardens* provides many practical tips on houseplant care, including both flowering and foliage plants, succulents, and a section on terrariums. Also included are sections on plant pests and ways of preventing and spotting problems, with useful charts making diagnosis simple. This booklet goes beyond basic ideas, however. Other chapters discuss display ideas, hardy uncommon houseplants, and forcing bulbs for a blooming winter season.

Send: $1.75

Ask for: C-35 "Houseplants"

Write to: National Plan Service, Inc.
435 W. Fullerton St.
Elmhurst, IL 60126

Greenhouse

To find out about a home addition that heats the house, grows plants, and provides a sun-basking area all year round, write for this informative brochure. The 14 pages include photographs, information, solar-energy heating charts, and more.

Send: $1.00

Ask for: The Four Seasons Passive Solar Greenhouse and Add-a-Room

Write to: Four Seasons Solar Products
910 Rt. 110
Farmingdale, NY 11735

XI.
Recipes and Home Storage

Come taste.

Build Your Own Cellar

If you are going to harvest your garden or backyard orchard, you will need a cool storage space. If you have the proper cellar, you can store a large supply of fruits and vegetables without refrigeration. This pamphlet includes information and plans for three types or locations of cellars—in a house basement, on level ground, or dug into a hillside.

Send: a self-addressed, stamped envelope

Ask for: "Building Your Own Cellar"

Write to: Information Officer
West Virginia Dept. of Agriculture
Capitol Building
Charleston, WV 25305

Home Dyeing with Natural Dyes

The renewed interest in handicraft work has led to a demand for information on how to dye materials with natural dyes. This reprint of a 1935 booklet by the Dept. of Agriculture gives just what you would need. Here are reliable data on the use of tree bark, nut hulls, and other natural dyestuffs. Learn what types of natural dyes you could gather locally in the region of the country where you live.

Send: $1.60

Ask for: "Home Dyeing with Natural Dyes"

Write to: Redwood City Seed Co.
P.O. Box 361
Redwood City, CA 94064

Canning

With the prices of fruits and vegetables skyrocketing these days, more and more people are returning to the old-fashioned method of canning their own and saving money during the long winter months. This government booklet contains 32 pages of recipes and canning techniques for a cornucopia of fruits and vegetables. Learn the secrets that Grandma used to keep the winter table filled with good wholesome meals…right from the cellar.

Send: $1.50

Ask for: "Home Canning of Fruits and Vegetables" (Home and Garden Bulletin 133J)

Write to: Consumer Information Center
Dept. Z
Pueblo, CO 81009

Drying Foods

Drying foods has been a way of preserving surplus food for thousands of years. Basically it entails reducing the moisture content to a level below which most molds and decay-causing organisms do not grow, but it means more than just leaving the food out of doors for sun-drying. The correct procedures for home-drying your produce are clearly explained in this pamphlet from the West Virginia Dept. of Agriculture.

Send: a self-addressed, stamped envelope

Ask for: "Drying Food"

Write to: Information Officer
West Virginia Dept. of Agriculture
Capitol Building
Charleston, WV 25305

Wild Recipes

This basic recipe book from Wild Things contains suggestions on how to include easily identifiable and tasty weeds, nuts, and berries in your daily menu. The many recipes include hors d'oeuvres, drinks, puddings, salads, and main courses. Order yours and discover what tasty dinners you could serve, garnished with the wild things that grow in your region.

Send: $2.00

Ask for: "Recipes from Wild Things"

Write to: Wild Things
P.O. Box 90
Covesville, VA 22931

Eat Wild Things

You may not want to follow in the tracks of Euell Gibbons, munching his way across America, but occasionally it is fun to include some natural food in your camp meals, food you pick along the trail. Here is a recipe book that teaches you what is safe and what is not, and how to incorporate the edible flora and plants into your diet. You'll find that there are many tasty weeds, berries, and nuts just waiting to be harvested.

Send: $2.00

Ask for: "Recipes from Wild Things"

Write to: Wild Things
P.O. Box 90
Covesville, VA 22931

Home Storage

Storage of fruits and vegetables was practiced extensively by our ancestors. All it really requires is an awareness of food characteristics that assist natural conditions. This brochure discusses various methods of preservation, and includes several comparative charts that assess the effectiveness of specific methods for individual fruits and vegetables. Also considered are outdoor and indoor storage structures, accompanied by construction plans. Specific storage conditions for over 25 fruits and vegetables are given.

Send: $1.25

Ask for: "Home Storage of Fresh Fruits and Vegetables"

Write to: Northeast Regional Agricultural Engineering Service
Riley Robb Hall
Cornell University,
Ithaca, NY 14853

Wine

"Cultural Practices for Commercial Vineyards" has useful advice for the serious amateur grape grower as well as the professional. This 70-page illustrated booklet discusses the grape industry in New York, selecting a site for your vineyard, planting the vineyard, controlling crop size, and discouraging pests. Also included is a discussion of the varieties of wine grapes, from pure American types to French-American and dessert grapes.

Send: $2.00

Ask for: "Cultural Practices for Commercial Vineyards"

Write to: Distribution Center C
7 Research Park
Cornell University
Ithaca, NY 14850

Root Cellars

There are low-cost ways to save your food supplies. Root cellars are one. Pits and trenches are others. This instructional book will tell you how to build your own root cellars, pits, and trenches. Also included are storage tips and advice on storage life expectancies for many fruits and vegetables.

Send: $2.00

Ask for: "Building and Using Your Root Cellar" (Garden Way Bulletin A-22)

Write to: Garden Way Publishing
Dept. A979
Charlotte, VT 05445

Home Canning

With more and more people planting home vegetable gardens, there has been a renewed interest in the old-fashioned tradition of canning the harvest at the end of the growing season. This pamphlet from the West Virginia Dept. of Agriculture explains the principles behind the canning process and shows you the techniques for boiling and sealing. Useful charts show the approximate yields.

Send: a self-addressed, stamped envelope

Ask for: "Successful Home Canning"

Write to: Information Officer
West Virginia Dept. of Agriculture
Capitol Building
Charleston, WV 25305

Storing Vegetables and Fruits

All those extra pounds of produce from your garden harvest will have to be stored someplace, and the traditional, time-tested places are cellars, outbuildings, and pits.

This 18-page government publication will tell you how to do it. In addition, you'll learn about keeping the storing place clean, maintaining proper moisture, and handling the produce.

Send: $2.00

Ask for: "Storing Vegetables and Fruits"
(Home and Garden Bulletin 135J)

Write to: Consumer Information Center
Dept. Z
Pueblo, CO 81009

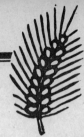

Grain Amaranths

Amaranths are fast-growing cereal-like plants that produce high-protein grains. Many developing countries are placing great hopes in their cultivation to improve the diets of their native populations. This booklet is a compendium of five articles exploring the many possible uses of this wonder plant, not only for the poorer nations of the world but even for America. Also included are several recipes using amaranth grains and amaranth greens.

Send: $1.05

Ask for: "Amaranth Round-up"

Write to: Redwood City Seed Co.
P.O. Box 361
Redwood City, CA 94064

Comprehensive Gardening

The Urban Gardening Program at Pennsylvania State University offers a comprehensive gardening program. Among their many available fliers are recipe sheets suggesting delightful ways of making use of your harvest. One page tells you how to make sweet-smelling potpourris and pomanders. Others suggest tasty mushroom and squash recipes. They also include out-of-the-ordinary weed recipes such as "Dandelion Roast" and "Clover Soup."

Send: a postcard

Ask for: recipe handout sheets

Write to: Urban Gardening Program
Pennsylvania State University
S.E. corner Broad and Grange Sts.
Philadelphia, PA 19141

Eat Wild Plants!

Yes, but only if you know which ones are edible. Our ancestors used dozens of wild plants collected over the four seasons of the year to enrich their daily fare, but such plant lore is gradually being forgotten by those of us who live in cities. If you want to "live off the land" on your next camping trip or merely season your normal meals with wild plants, order this handy pamphlet and discover which of the plants you have been hiking past all these years could become part of your evening dinner.

Send: a self-addressed, stamped envelope

Ask for: "Edible Wild Plants"

Write to: Information Officer
West Virginia Dept. of Agriculture
Capitol Building
Charleston, WV 25305

Build Your Own Root Cellar

This booklet presents step-by-step instructions for constructing a root cellar to store your harvest. Alternative structures for small-scale storage are also included. The crucial factors of temperature, humidity, and ventilation are discussed, as are the issues of siting, insulating, and actual storing. If you dry, cook, and freeze each fall to preserve your fresh produce, perhaps it's time to consider this natural option.

Send: $1.75

Ask for: "How to Build and Use a Root Cellar"

Write to: Butterbrooke Farm
78 Barry Rd.
Oxford, CT 06483

XII.
For the Armchair Gardener:
Books and Publications

Add Hours to Your Flowers

Who doesn't want to know how to extend the life of cut flowers? This brochure from the New York State College of Agriculture and Life Sciences explains in 10 easy steps the basic procedure for prolonging the life of cut flowers. Each step is accompanied by a photograph.

Send: free to residents of New York State; 20¢ elsewhere

Ask for: "Add Hours to Your Flowers"

Write to: Distribution Center C
7 Research Park
Cornell University
Ithaca, NY 14850

Seed Self-Reliance

From Butterbrooke Farm comes a super gardener's how-to on completing nature's life cycle. This flier is an easy-to-understand

guide that explains the advance planning necessary to harvest, dry, and store seeds from your own garden. Also included is an explanation of annual, biennial, and perennial seeds and their effect on your hobby.

Send: 75¢

Ask for: "How to Save Seed from Your Own Garden Produce"

Write to: Butterbrooke Farm
78 Barry Rd.
Oxford, CT 06483

Books for Gardeners

The 1982 edition of Capability's "Books for Gardeners" contains over 400 titles spread over 48 pages. The titles cover a wide variety of topics: indoor, outdoor, vegetable, hydroponic, and flower gardening; plant photography; landscape gardening; birds; as well as specialty books on roses, cacti, orchids, trees, shrubs, wild flowers, ferns, and many more. A special section on cooking and preserving vegetables is also included. The $1.00 charge is refundable with the first order.

Send: $1.00

Ask for: "Capability's Books for Gardeners"

Write to: Capability's Books for Gardeners
Hwy. 46
Rt. 1, P.O. Box 114
Deer Park, WI 54007

The Outdoor Urban Garden

The urban gardener with a community plot is faced with many problems. Inadequate soil nutrients and water supply are among the most prominent. The Urban Gardening Program offers very useful handout sheets on just these problems. Ideas for economical composting are suggested, as well as a number of irrigation systems. Also included are excellent water-saving suggestions.

Send: a postcard

Ask for: "Garden Structures" handout sheets

Write to: Urban Gardening Program
Pennsylvania State University
S.E. corner Broad and Grange Sts.
Philadelphia, PA 19141

Know-How

"The Know-How Catalog" offers you free or inexpensive bulletins, leaflets, booklets, packets, and other printed material from the New York State College of Human Ecology and the New York State College of Agriculture and Life Sciences at Cornell University. Topics covered include Fruit—Production and Storage, Ornamental Horticulture, Soil Management, Vegetable Production, Pest Control, Beekeeping, and many others. The catalog is clearly presented and indexed, making it simple to find exactly what you're looking for.

Send: a postcard

Ask for: "The Know-How Catalog"

Write to: Distribution Center C
7 Research Park
Cornell University
Ithaca, NY 14850

Mother's Bookshelf

Who can you trust for reliable information on gardening, greenhouses, herbs? Who but Mother. "Mother's Bookshelf" from *The Mother Earth News* offers selected books on every aspect of gardening. From *The Foolproof Gardening Guide* to *Planning Your Garden: A Visual Guide*. From *Better Vegetable Gardens the Chinese Way* to *Building and Using a Solar-Heated Geodesic Greenhouse*, Mother offers the very best guides reliably and inexpensively. You'll want to have a look at their chock-full catalog.

Send: $1.00

Ask for: "Mother's Bookshelf"

Write to: The Retail Book Division
The Mother Earth News, Inc.
P.O. Box 70
Hendersonville, NC 28791

School Gardens

School gardens can be living laboratories where children can delight in nature and learn the subtle whys and wherefores of the good earth. Teach children about natural cycles and ecological relationships with a garden planted and tended by them somewhere on the school property. This brochure will give you step-by-step instructions for planting a garden from start to finish, at the same time suggesting other references you may want to use.

Send: 25¢ and a self-addressed, stamped envelope

Ask for: "School Gardens"

Write to: Sierra Club
530 Bush St.
San Francisco, CA 94108

Gardening for the Beginner

Here is a primer for basic gardening. Learn the basics that will let you start a garden simply and inexpensively. This pamphlet tells you how to select a garden site, how to prepare the soil, choose the right seeds and tools, and how to arrange your garden. Once it's all planted, you'll learn how to control weeds and insects. Don't let the mysteries of gardening scare you off. It's easier than you think!

Send: a self-addressed, stamped envelope

Ask for: "Home Gardening Is Fun"

Write to: Information Officer
West Virginia Dept. of Agriculture
Capitol Building
Charleston, WV 25305

A Child's Garden

This little booklet is designed for both adult and child gardeners and offers a bounty of suggestions for ways to share the joy and excitement of growing things with your young ones. Single copies free to teachers, 50¢ to individuals. Quantity orders are less.

Send: 50¢ (teachers send a postcard)

Ask for: "A Child's Garden"

Write to: Chevron Chemical Co.
Educational Materials
Public Affairs Dept.
P.O. Box 3744
San Francisco, CA 94119

Send: $1.00

Ask for: "Calendar of Wild Things"

Write to: Wild Things
P.O. Box 90
Covesville, VA 22931

Calendar

Here is a postcard-size calendar of illustrations from Wild Things, the people who teach you how to eat the wild plants, weeds, berries, and nuts that nature provides. Pictures are of some of the Wild Things people's favorite wild things. You'll like them too!

Gardening Questions?

Get some answers. And here they are! Arranged in handy charts and listings to cover all the many types of plants and soils and problems that arise in the average garden. Planting dates, insects, leftover seeds, mulching, manures, and harvesting. And frost, transplanting, cultivating, and types of tomatoes. And much more!

Send: $2.00

Ask for: "Gardening Answers" (Garden Way Bulletin A-49)

Write to: Garden Way Publishing
Dept. A979
Charlotte, VT 05445

Honeybee

The honeybee is a fascinating insect, both fearsome and sweet. This booklet includes an overview of the history of beekeeping, and a discussion of the life stages of the bee supplemented by explanatory drawings. Although not a how-to for aspiring bee-keepers, it is a fine introduction to the subject.

Send: $1.50

Ask for: "Understanding the Honey Bee"

Write to: The Bio-Dynamic Farming and Gardening Association, Inc.
P.O. Box 253
Wyoming, RI 02898

Garden Shows

The Urban Gardening Program offers helpful information for every gardener entering gardening contests. The program will send you handout sheets with great tips for keeping your flowers and vegetables fresh looking, or how to be sure your plants will be fully ripe or in bloom the day of the competition. These sheets are a must for any competitive gardener.

Send: a postcard

Ask for: "Harvesting the Garden" handout sheets

Write to: Urban Gardening Program
Pennsylvania State University
S.E. corner Broad and Grange Sts.
Philadelphia, PA 19141

Plant Guide

Geraniums just might qualify as America's favorite flower, The USDA census of 1979 counted 47 million geraniums grown by flower lovers. Here is a flower guidebook specializing in geraniums, African violets, and other houseplants. It also has a page of special plants, most of which are less than $2.00 each.

Send: a postcard

Ask for: "Plant Guide"

Write to: Wilson Brothers Floral Co.
Roachdale, IN 46172

Shade Tree Care

It pays to keep your shade trees healthy and alive. Shade and ornamental trees add beauty and value to your property. If you fail to maintain your shade trees, your property value will decline and your home may actually suffer damage from falling limbs or, what's worse, a falling tree. Remember that when a tree is lost due to lack of care, you lose money and beauty. Learn how to keep your trees beautiful and healthy.

Send: a self-addressed, stamped envelope

Ask for: "Shade Tree Care"

Write to: Information Officer
West Virginia Dept. of Agriculture
Capitol Building
Charleston, WV 25305

Plants for Difficult Situations

This excellent pamphlet printed by the University of Connecticut lists shrubs, vines, perennials, annuals, and trees suitable for all kinds of climate and soil types. Pesticide safety tips are also included.

Send: 25¢

Ask for: "Plants for Difficult Situations"

Write to: Cooperative Extension Service
College of Agriculture and Natural Resources
The University of Connecticut
Storrs, CT 06268

Poison Ivy

Poison ivy has many disguises. The old proverb "leaflets three, let it be" is true, but people still mistake harmless plants for the real villain and blithely tromp through thick patches of poison ivy without noticing it. This pamphlet will show you with illustrations the various guises of this pesky little plant, along with its obnoxious cousins poison oak and poison sumac.

Send: a self-addressed, stamped envelope

Ask for: "Poison Ivy and Its Control"

Write to: Information Officer
West Virginia Dept. of Agriculture
Capitol Building
Charleston, WV 25305

Gardening for Beginners

The Urban Gardening Program at Pennsylvania State University offers the basics for beginning gardeners in urban or rural regions. These handout sheets discuss soil alkalinity, seeding, transplanting vegetables, the comparative needs of vegetables, early and late planting, and much else. Individual sheets are also available on growing bean sprouts, celery, peanuts, soybeans, sweet potatoes, winter greens, peaches, and geraniums. These sheets contain direct, easy-to-understand, and useful information. None better for the beginner.

Send: a postcard

Ask for: "Garden Know-How" handout sheets

Write to: The Urban Gardening Program
Pennsylvania State University
S.E. corner Broad and Grange Sts.
Philadelphia, PA 19141

Trees for a More Livable Environment

This little booklet looks at trees in a very special way—as resources, tools to use to make a more livable environment. Charts abound, and lists of trees for special situations are included. Single copies free.

Send: a postcard

Ask for: "Trees for a More Livable Environment"

Write to: Chevron Chemical Co.
Educational Materials
Public Affairs Dept.
P.O. Box 3744
San Francisco, CA 94119

Plants with Poisonous Properties

This leaflet was written with gardeners, parents, teachers, doctors, camp counselors, scout and 4-H leaders, and health professionals in mind. It lists rules to follow to avoid accidental poisoning and what to do in case poisoning occurs. Hundreds of poisonous plants, trees, shrubs, flowers, and seeds are listed, with a description of the poisonous item as well as the symptoms to be alert for.

Send: 50¢

Ask for: "Plants with Poisonous Properties"

Write to: Cooperative Extension Service
College of Agriculture and Natural Resources
The University of Connecticut
Storrs, CT 06268

Useful Plants

This catalog of useful plants is an encyclopedia of information for the home gardener. It's arranged alphabetically by topic (vegetables, herbs, fruits-nut-berries, dye plants, and various plants), so you'll be able to go immediately to the plant that you're interested in. Also included is a list of books on the many aspects of gardening. All plants and books can be ordered by mail.

Send: 75¢

Ask for: "Catalog of Useful Plants"

Write to: Redwood City Seed Co.
P.O. Box 361
Redwood City, CA 94064

Know Your Poisonous Plants

Any plant that upsets your normal health is dangerous and considered poisonous. Whether it be a skin rash, a burning sensation, or stomach trouble after you eat them (such as mushrooms), you have been poisoned. Learn which plants are dangerous and how to avoid them. Common, household first-aid treatments are also suggested.

Send: a self-addressed, stamped envelope

Ask for: "Poisonous Plants"

Write to: Information Officer
West Virginia Dept. of Agriculture
Capitol Building
Charleston, WV 25305

Make Your Own Corsages

Corsages can be made inexpensively and easily. "Corsages from Garden Flowers" tells you how. This booklet explains the assembly of corsages: how to wire the flowers, how to tape them, and how to make the perfect bow. Suggestions on how to wear corsages are included, as is a list of garden flowers that make pretty corsages. Instructions for assembling spray corsages are also given.

Send: 25¢

Ask for: "Corsages from Garden Flowers"

Write to: Distribution Center C
7 Research Park
Cornell University
Ithaca, NY 14850

Everything You Wanted to Know About Seeds

This fascinating guide to seeds will be a boon to anyone's gardening library. The life stages of seeds are discussed, as well as advice on growing and saving your own seeds. Also included are several lists comparing life span, weight, gathering time. You'll find old gardening myths dispelled in this pamphlet.

Send: $1.50

Ask for: "From Seed to Seed"

Write to: The Bio-Dynamic Farming and
Gardening Association, Inc.
P.O. Box 253
Wyoming, RI 02898

Vegetables Made Easy!

This pamphlet for beginners will tell you how to plant and care for common garden vegetables—corn, potatoes, tomatoes, cabbage, peppers, cucumbers, lettuce, beans, onions, carrots, pumpkins, radishes, peas, carrots, beets, and zucchini. Learn how to start your garden with these vegetables, how to prepare the soil after selecting the site, and, most important, how to design your garden on paper before you ever lift a shovel.

Send: a self-addressed, stamped envelope

Ask for: "Gardening for Beginners"

Write to: Information Officer
West Virginia Dept. of Agriculture
Capitol Building
Charleston, WV 25305

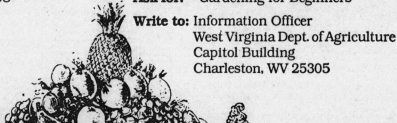

Ken Druse is an award winning gardening writer
and photographer. His work has appeared in
numerous general and specialty publications.